Gulpilil

Derek Rielly

MACMILLAN
Pan Macmillan Australia

Aboriginal and Torres Strait Islander people should be aware that this book may contain images or names of people now deceased.

First published 2019 in Macmillan by Pan Macmillan Australia Pty Ltd
1 Market Street, Sydney, New South Wales, Australia, 2000

Copyright © Derek Rielly 2019

The moral right of the author to be identified as the author of this work has been asserted.

All rights reserved. No part of this book may be reproduced or transmitted by any person or entity (including Google, Amazon or similar organisations), in any form or by any means, electronic or mechanical, including photocopying, recording, scanning or by any information storage and retrieval system, without prior permission in writing from the publisher.

Cataloguing-in-Publication entry is available
from the National Library of Australia
http://catalogue.nla.gov.au

Typeset in 10/14pt Chronicle Text by Post Pre-press Group, Brisbane
Internal design by Daniel New
Photography by Richard Freeman
Printed by McPherson's Printing Group

Excerpts from *Charlie's Country* press notes on pages 7–8, 18, *The Tracker* production notes on pages 111–12, *The Tracker* on pages 190, 228 and 229 used with kind permission from Rolf de Heer, all rights reserved. *The Tracker* image on page 5 of picture insert used with kind permission from Rolf de Heer, all rights reserved.
Excerpts from *Gulpilil: the one-man show* on pages ix, 7, 44, 122, 123–24 and 129–30 used with kind permission from Reg Cribb, all rights reserved.
Excerpts from *Why Warriors Lay Down and Die* on pages 16, 198, 199 and 205 used with kind permission from Richard Trudgen, all rights reserved.
Image of *Two Worlds* on page 10 of picture insert used with kind permission from Craig Ruddy, all rights reserved.

The author and the publisher have made every effort to contact copyright holders for material used in this book. Any person or organisation that may have been overlooked should contact the publisher.

MIX
Paper from responsible sources
FSC® C001695

The paper in this book is FSC® certified. FSC® promotes environmentally responsible, socially beneficial and economically viable management of the world's forests.

Gulpilil

Also by Derek Rielly

Wednesdays with Bob

For Gard, for Jones, for Shawnee,
for love and for home ...

Contents

1:	Finding Home	1
2:	The Movie Star and the Nurse	11
3:	My Brother Jack	23
4:	Gulpilil vs Dennis Hopper	39
5:	The Queers on the Hill	49
6:	Gulpilil Wins the Archibald	57
7:	A Famous Artist Paints a Portrait of the Old Man	73
8:	Paul Hogan Goes to an Alice Springs Casino, Meets Gulpilil	95
9:	The Fanatic, The Follower and The Tracker	105
10:	Gulpilil: The One-Man Show	119
11:	As Moodoo in Rabbit-Proof Fence	133
12:	Battle of the Ancestors	147
13:	The Handler	159
14:	A Photo Shoot at Poverty Corner	171
15:	A Film Critic Discusses Gulpilil's Movies	187
16:	From Dreams to Nightmares	195
17:	Jack Says Goodbye	211
18:	The Week Before Christmas	215
	Endnotes	231
	Acknowledgements	243

Acting came natural to me. Piece of piss. I know how to walk across the land in front of a camera because I belong there.

From the one-man show, *Gulpilil*, 2004

CHAPTER 1

Finding Home

SEVENTY-SEVEN KILOMETRES SOUTHEAST OF Adelaide on the Princes Highway to Melbourne, the blooming hills give way to a flat plain and a city of seventeen thousand souls called Murray Bridge.

For the Ngarrindjeri, Aboriginal people of the lower Murray River and surrounds, which include the beaches of the Coorong where *Storm Boy* (1976) was shot, it's Pomberuk.

It's significant country. All eighteen clans that made up the Ngarrindjeri people would meet at Murray Bridge for corroborees. Down the road at Tailem Bend, the clans would trade.

Ngarrindjeri man David Unaipon, inventor, writer, authority on ballistics and face of the fifty-dollar bill, Australia's Leonardo da Vinci it's said, was born nearby in 1872 and died in Tailem Bend hospital ninety-four years later.

In 2019, a de facto 'Welcome to Murray Bridge' sign is the sandstone White Hill Truck Drivers Memorial, the ghostly rigs of 105 dead truckers presented in relief and dedicated to two-year-old Tamika Hourn and her one-year-old brother Khaleb, who died in a truck crash on Easter Monday in 1995.

Tailem Bend is home to Old Tailem Town, 'Australia's largest pioneer village', where you can 'walk back down memory lane in the most realistic surroundings possible'.

Murray Bridge has one broad strip called Adelaide Road. A tattoo shop offers Vape 'hardware and juice' and numbing cream for twenty dollars, with a five-dollar discount per tube if the tattoo is completed on premises. Saturday night welcomes a Tom Jones tribute show to Murray Bridge Town Hall, with tables of ten available for three hundred dollars. A giant white elephant, its mouth fashioned into a smile, sits on its haunches atop *Daish Irrigation and Fodder*.

Fast-food joints, service stations and motels feed and shelter the weary traveller, usually heading either west to Adelaide or across the border into Victoria. Australian cars from the nineteen-nineties, whose after-market exhaust pipes have mouths like hungry gropers, sit in servo car parks. They are slow to start on the cold mornings, but erupt suddenly and with vigour, shaking the occupants.

Murray Bridge, therefore, is an Australian country town like most.

Slow. A little wary. On the poor side, but the people have a roof over their heads, a cheap car in the driveway, a river to slosh around in, enough to eat.

Too hot in summer; an ice-box in winter.

Eighty grand buys a thousand square metres of land; one-fifty and you're in a pretty three-bedroom house that'd deliver very little change from two mill in Sydney.

And it's here in Murray Bridge, past the XD Falcon that's been converted into a hearse and has the licence plate RIP, and in a block of sandstone townhouses wrapped in aprons of faux-colonial decoration, down a battle-axe driveway and three and a half thousand kilometres from his community of Ramingining in Arnhem Land, we find the final home of a Yolngu man, the Australian actor David Gulpilil.

Gulpilil.

Forget David, the Christian, or if we want to be historically accurate, Hebrew, name missionaries gave him.

Or if you really want to peel away history, the second name he copped from the white, or what the Yolngu call Balanda, world.

'At first my name was Joe,' Gulpilil told the ABC in 1978. 'Then I went to the welfare school which is the welfare settlement and they asked me what was my name. And I said my name is Gulpilil. And suddenly they said, "All right we'll give you David."'

Either way. Forget it.

Gulpilil.

The British got Jagger; the Americans, Elvis.

Australia has the Original.

A man above everything and everyone, a living connection to a sixty-thousand-year cultural continuum. Born in 1953, or thereabouts, in a region so remote he didn't see a white man until he was eight, to parents who still carried the memory of pastoral massacres. Like all tribal Aboriginal people, missionaries gave him the birth date of 1 July, the first day of the financial year.

Gulpilil is dangerous good looks strapped to a lean musculature with only the essential flesh, bone and skin. A bushel of swashbuckling hair, an impossible-to-mimic walk and bow-tied with the ability to silently tell a story with movements of his face.

What does Gulpilil evoke for you?

Do you remember when he came into your life? Was it a cinema or TV showing of Nicolas Roeg's *Walkabout* (1971) on a Saturday night, Gulpilil's first moment on screen a close-up of his iliac furrow, the so-called Adonis belt, naked but for a braided leather belt holding a trio of dead goannas?

Did you cower during Gulpilil's climactic mating dance for the topless Jenny Agutter, as arousing as it was terrifying?

Or when her rejection drove him to suicide?

Was it the first time you'd seen an Aboriginal portrayed not as the yes-boss-yes-boss savage desperate for salvation from his white master, but as a powerful and... *superior*... being?

'Let's talk about *Walkabout*,' says an American reporter in 1979, melting before this gorgeous man smiling in front of her. 'You were wonderful, it was beautiful and you moved like a *gazelle...*'

Maybe it was his Billy alongside Dennis Hopper's title role in *Mad Dog Morgan* (1976)? The director and writer Philippe Mora wrote Gulpilil into the movie, long before the American was cast, because of his 'magic' in *Walkabout*.

'I think he's fantastic and I still do,' says Mora. 'He's a director's dream. There aren't many people the camera loves, and this is going to be a strange comparison, but Marilyn Monroe had the same quality. She couldn't take a bad photograph. And I don't think you could film David badly. My god, his face is a novel.'

Or as Fingerbone Bill in the movie version of Colin Thiele's 1963 novella *Storm Boy* when he teaches a kid how to live and a father how to love?

Like Mora, director Peter Weir also wrote Gulpilil into a film, the climate change apocalypse *The Last Wave*, which starred American actor Richard Chamberlain alongside Gulpilil's mystical Chris Lee, after a conversation with Gulpilil in a bar.

It was the first time the director of *Picnic at Hanging Rock* and *The Cars That Ate Paris* had ever done such a thing.

'It's dangerous: you might not be able to get the person,' said Weir in a 1979 interview shortly after *The Last Wave*'s release. '[But] ... he said some things about his family and then suddenly he said some English sentence. It was something like "You see my father and I, and that's why because the moon isn't."'

Weir asked Gulpilil to repeat the sentence, which he did ... twice. It didn't help. Weir left the riddle hanging, circulating, in his head for a night and day.

'Suddenly I realised what it was. That he was talking about another perception ... That was a breakthrough for me ... because then I would look out for these moments or I would provoke them.'

Or maybe your first experience of Gulpilil wasn't quite so profound?

Was it his comedic turn as Neville Bell in *Crocodile Dundee* (1986) when he tells the New York reporter she can't take his photo?

'I'm sorry – because you think it will take your spirit away,' she asks.

'Nah, you've got lens cap on,' laughs Gulpilil.

Gulpilil's career, his most vital roles, can be traced alongside the trajectory of white–black relations in Australia.

In the program for Gulpilil's one-man show at the Adelaide Festival in 2004, *Gulpilil*, the playwright Reg Cribb notes:

> **He has been viewed with suspicion and fear by his own people for becoming a 'spoilt' blackfella and our film industry has at times treated his culture and wisdom carelessly and left him wondering what, at the end of the day, does he have to give back to his own people? David's story, in many ways, *is* the Aboriginal story.**

In *Walkabout*, Gulpilil saves the lost white kids while he's destroyed.

In *Charlie's Country* (2013), which is set during 2007's 'Northern Territory Emergency Response' or 'Intervention', Gulpilil as 'Charlie' tries to go back to the old ways but finds his ability to survive in the bush has evaporated after generations of white interference.

'My friend David Gulpilil is a troubled soul,' writes the director Rolf de Heer in his press notes for *Charlie's Country*.

> **I sometimes liken his plight to that of the great Australian painter Albert Namatjira, who was likewise unable to**

reconcile the two cultures he had to live in, his own, and ours... Remarkably though, it's a film that speaks as loudly for David the man as it does for David the actor. He goes through deep emotion when watching it... he laughs, he trembles on the brink of crying, and the politics of it make him angry with the world.

'He has a foot in both cultures. It's an enormous strain on the man,' says Peter Weir in his 1979 interview. '[He] is torn, and he has broken his tribal law by moving to the city, by marrying a black girl who is not tribal. He goes home, they still accept him in his tribal area, but he's under enormous tension. It's impossible to know what tension he's under.'

An early scene in *Charlie's Country* shows Gulpilil shouting in his language, Yolngu Matha, outside the newly installed cop station in Ramingining.

Translated: 'You come from far away and bring us alcohol, ganja, tobacco... all bad!'

A cop, who doesn't understand the language of the people he's been brought in to police, to make 'em register their old jalopies, to confiscate their spears, to make 'em register their guns, steps outside to examine the source of the noise.

'G'day Luke!' says Gulpilil, brightly.

'G'day Charlie!' says the cop.

'You white bastard.'

'You black bastard.'

Cue a volcano of Gulpilil's falsetto laughter, a friendly tilt of the head and a wave of his finger. The role would win him the Best Actor award at Un Certain Regard in 2014, an offshoot of the Cannes Film Festival.

Could more fitting metaphors for Indigenous Australia be constructed?

The pain of an ancient culture, the inability of the dominant culture to understand or appreciate the people they've subjugated, and the artificial smiles from both.

Three years after his Cannes win, Gulpilil began to vomit uncontrollably at night. There were panicked late-night hospital visits. Then came a terrible pain in his right shoulder.

The first doctor gave him the anti-inflammatory drug Voltaren and told him to go home. Other doctors blew it off after examining his throat, stomach, gut and bowels with an endoscopy and a colonoscopy, with varying diagnoses – a stomach ulcer, and so on.

Gulpilil's carer joked that if it did turn out to be a stomach ulcer it was only because he'd been gobbling the Voltaren like candy.

Finally, a senior doctor said he'd keep investigating until he found the cause.

It didn't take much. One X-ray of his lungs revealed multiple shadows.

Lung cancer.

Gulpilil asked, 'Can't you cut it out?'

The doctor said there were too many tumours.

He was told he should prepare to cash out in six, maybe eight months. Give up the ganja and it might buy him a little more time.

Still, Gulpilil should've been dead in September 2017.

Almost two years later, he's still here.

CHAPTER 2

The Movie Star and the Nurse

A WOMAN OF FOUR FEET AND EIGHT INCHES with a Cromwell helmet of silvered hair and small rectangular glasses, dressed in blue jeans and sweater and wearing chocolate brown ankle-length Ugg boots, swings the security door open.

Welcome Mary Hood, Gulpilil's carer for the last two years, a sixty-nine-year-old former aged care nurse from South Australia whose love of the desert ('It has my heart') and the Aboriginal world sent her to Darwin. A super-hero in the very ordinary sense of one loving human who welcomed a troubled man, and his now estranged wife, Miriam, into her little Darwin house after she met 'em both at the premiere of *Ten Canoes* in 2006.

In 2011, Gulpilil was sentenced to twelve months jail for breaking Miriam's arm in a boozy fight. The court heard that he'd thrown a broom at her, breaking her arm, when she refused get off the floor and come to him while drinking at a house in Darwin. He was short of friends, so it was Mary who went to visit. When he'd done his time, the parole officer asked if Mary, who lived with an Aboriginal family, would take him.

Gulpilil had stopped drinking in prison and was still with Miriam, who'd told the court that she regretted reporting the incident to police.

But he didn't want to return with Miriam to their life of drunkenness in Darwin's infamous Long Grass bush camps. In a story from 2013, journalist Paul Toohey described a lawless world where women slept with knives for protection and traded sex for a box of moselle, a packet of smokes, a phone card or some ganja. The women, wrote Toohey, felt excluded from society and enjoyed 'travelling in nice cars or, on rare occasions, being taken to private homes with stocked fridges and showers.'

'It was a temporary escape, and a better deal, than the routine rape they suffered at the hands of their own men.

'One woman said: "The blackfellas sneak up on you when you are passed out, alone, and do their thing and leave. Then another one comes and climbs on. And another."'

Mary being Mary – she's seen everything, and isn't one to judge or hold a grudge – welcomed Gulpilil and his wife.

'Come and stay and Nana will look after you,' she'd told Miriam.

But after a Saturday night or two, says Mary, 'The grog would call her back to the Long Grass.'

In 2015, Mary, a mother of four who'd split from her husband back in 1993, got injured, and then sick, and figured, I'm in my sixties, maybe it's time I retired. Gulpilil drove Mary the three thousand kilometres from Darwin to Adelaide so she could look for a new place to call home.

Drove her back to Darwin to pack her things.

Three times this unlikely pair, the movie star and the retired nurse, did the six-thousand-kilometre round-trip.

'He doesn't stop for anything,' says Mary. 'Full-steam ahead. On that first trip we left at lunchtime on a Friday and we were at my sister's place at Murray Bridge by nine on Sunday night.'

There were moments.

Mary talks about the time Gulpilil stopped when he saw some Aboriginal girls trying to hunt. He jumped out of the old red

LandCruiser – which blew so much smoke they avoided major towns like Katherine and Tennant Creek 'because the cops would've pulled us over straight away' – found a goanna's hole, grabbed its fugitive and expertly killed it.

'With his hands!' says Mary. 'The girls were happy. They had some tucker and then off we went.'

Eighteen months after Mary had found a small townhouse in Murray Bridge, Gulpilil called and said, 'Mary, book me a flight tomorrow morning. I'm coming to live with you.'

He hasn't been back to Darwin, or Ramingining, since.

One step inside the three-bedder and I walk straight into the iconic face.

'I'm David Gulpilil! Ha! Ha!' he hoots. 'Been here a couple of years now. I come from the Northern Territory. Arnhem Land!'

Riven by nerves, by the proximity of the great actor, his face still beautiful, body a featherweight fifty-nine kilos, a sudden, prolonged silence and the knowledge of his diagnosis, I blurt, 'You have cancer . . . uh . . . do you feel okay?'

I'm an idiot, a clown in oversized boots stomping blindly over any sort of cultural sensitivities.

'Uh, okay, yeah.'

What sort of cancer is it?

'Lung, isn't it David,' says Mary, acutely aware that Gulpilil is conversing in his sixth language, as well as being terribly ill.

The language of Gulpilil's father is Mandhalpingu, his mother, Ganalbingu. If you want to count 'em, he says he speaks fourteen: Dabi, Djinang, Wulaki, Djambarrpuyngu, Gupapuyngu, and so on.

Gulpilil wheezes.

'Yeah, lung. *Both lungs,*' he says.

Does it hurt to breathe?

'Yeah, sometimes it hurts.'

Mary senses my awkwardness. Later, she'll pull me aside and gently tell me to read the book, *Why Warriors Lie Down and Die* by Richard Trudgen.

'It will help you,' she says.

From the chapter 'Communication Mores':

> **Yolngu are taught to speak indirectly to a person with almost no eye contact ... Yolngu practise active listening ... this means that Yolngu people, in general, will not start to think about a response until the speaker has finished and they have heard what is being said ... Yolngu are taught from birth to think carefully about what they are going to say before they say it.**

Gulpilil looks at me sideways, his dark eyes ringed by blue cataracts.

'So I have to write a book before I go!' he grins. 'I want to write this book before I go!'

Gulpilil stands supported by a carved wooden cane, a gift from a new friend in Murray Bridge, Terry Hocking, who threw Gulpilil a sixty-fifth birthday bash six weeks earlier on his property a little up the road.

He has a beard and moustache, which is mostly grey, with a few black cameos. His hair is long and straight and hangs across his chest.

'The chemo took out the curls,' says Mary.

Gulpilil wears a black sleeveless jacket over a purple checked shirt, T-shirt and black jeans with comfortable black shoes.

His hands are like nothing I've seen before. From regular-sized pads sprout thick, powerful fingers, each appendage crowned by a curved fingernail that has the appearance of being painted in metallic gold nail polish.

The index finger of his right is abbreviated at the final knuckle.

'Amputated,' he says. 'A drum got me. Forty-four-gallon drum. Long time ago. Sixty-nine.'

We sit in the front room that is four-metres-by-three-metres in front of a gas fire to ward off the early spring chill and a television that is left on. A three-seater floral couch butts up against one wall; two floral lounge chairs face the TV, arm-rests pushed together.

Gulpilil sits in one, Mary the other.

Five minutes before he wakes each morning Mary will switch on the heater and television.

It's a little after midday. Gulpilil has been awake for an hour.

A certificate commemorating his prize for best actor for *Charlie's Country* at Cannes is framed and mounted on the wall. Alongside are government certificates for the registration of his company, Gulpilil Pty Ltd.

A table next to a television sitting on a carved wooden plinth displays a photo of his sister Yvonne, daughter Makia and his twin sister, Mary, who played a small role in the movie *Ten Canoes* alongside his son Jamie.

Gulpilil has four kids, two boys and two girls – Jida, Makia, Jamie and Phoebe – to four different mothers.

Significant women in Gulpilil's life are Diana Murray (mother of Jida), Jill Ganindjar (mother of Jamie), the white nurse Airlie Thomas who lived with Gulpilil in Ramingining and Marwuyu Gulparil from 1990 to 1993, the Indigenous artist Robyn Djunginy, a tribal woman whom Gulpilil lived with for fifteen years, and the aforementioned Miriam Ashley.

We see a photo of David with a pelican; a still from 2003's *The Tracker* with its director Rolf de Heer. There's his 2013 Red Ochre Award, which is a gold plate, for 'keeping culture strong' alongside a poster from the Australian embassy in Manila for a showing of the documentary *Crocodile Dreaming* that reads, 'In honour of visiting Australian actor Mr David Gulpilil, OAM'.

In the poster's photograph, Gulpilil, who had just completed de Heer's *Charlie's Country*, is unrecognisable. He is besuited, his face is shaved and he has close-cropped hair.

De Heer describes a meeting with Gulpilil in the low-security unit of Darwin's Berrimah prison, in his press notes for *Charlie's Country*:

> One of my thoughts had been, what can I do to help David? What can anybody do? A visit is a fine thing, but unless there are some possibilities for the road ahead, it doesn't amount to much. Unless I were to change my life, however, move up to Darwin to help him find his way, that sort of thing, there was little I could do for him. And even that would probably achieve little but heartbreak.
>
> I realised that the only thing I might be able to do for him was to make a film with him. It might give him a renewed sense of purpose, of belief in himself. It might just help set him on a different road, be useful as a transition to a more ordered life. It'd give him something to look forward to.
>
> Though apparently much improved compared to when he was imprisoned (he had weighed only 39 kgs by then), David looked pretty awful . . . khaki shorts, thongs and olive green T-shirt (David can be a snappy dresser), short hair (good for the climate but very un-David), expression pretty-well lifeless (David is one of the most fiercely alive people I've met). I feared for him, understood that he must have been severely depressed, and why wouldn't he be, considering where he was and what was ahead of him?

Gulpilil looks at me, suddenly embarrassed.

'Watching TV. I'm boring,' he says.

Conversation is difficult. I was told by de Heer before I came that I'd be lucky to get a dozen words out of Gulpilil. I figure by visiting regularly, by talking to actors, directors, friends and so on who know him well, I can create a picture of who Gulpilil is and why he matters, why he ... *still* ... matters.

Phillip Noyce went to film school with Gulpilil in 1973, and almost thirty years later, after a string of Hollywood blockbuster films starring the likes of Michael Caine, Harrison Ford and James Earl Jones, he directed Gulpilil in *Rabbit-Proof Fence*. Noyce describes Gulpilil's ability to see white and black, the future and the present, simultaneously.

'He's in a league of his own,' says Noyce.

Most days Gulpilil and Mary go for a drive to the river. Or to a cafe for barramundi and chips. Every few weeks, the documentary-maker Molly Reynolds (whose doco *Another Country* examines, through Gulpilil, the impact of white culture on his community, Ramingining – 'This film is about what happened to *my* culture,' he says, 'when it was interrupted by *your* culture') and her husband Rolf de Heer arrive from their home in Tasmania to shoot interviews for a documentary of Gulpilil's last days. The film will be released when he dies.

Gulpilil takes me on a tour of the house, which is so compact that I've seen everything in a couple of minutes. He shows me a poster-sized photograph of his role in *The Tracker*, his neck yoked by metal bolt to his white master. Another photo, this time from *Walkabout*.

A witch doll hangs from the roof.

I point at it. *You?*

'Ha! Ha! It's Mary!' says Gulpilil.

A letter from the Premier of South Australia, Steve Marshall, is framed and mounted on a wall next to the dining table:

> **I understand you are fighting a mighty battle with cancer and you continue to defy! Nothing would surprise me given your extraordinary spirit ... Go well Mr Gulpilil and know**

that your legacy will continue to be honoured and respected by us all.

Back in the front room, I ask to take photos.

Mary and David sitting alongside each other in their lounge chairs. A close-up of the famous face. Of those emu-like fingers with the fine gold fingernails.

We discuss the idea of a book, something, surprisingly, that has never come, despite Gulpilil's body of work. Mary tells me he has Fridays and Saturdays free. On Wednesdays, she drives him into Adelaide for immunotherapy treatment.

'Waiting, waiting, waiting,' says Gulpilil.

He yawns.

This is Mary's cue to ask Gulpilil about the book, about me. My visit is to see if we fit. To see if Gulpilil is comfortable with this white fella coming in to tell his story.

'What do you think, Old Man? Do you like Derek? Do you want to do this book?'

(Mary will pull me aside afterwards and explain, 'By the way, I'm not being rude calling him Old Man. It's like calling you sir or gentleman. I have to explain because some people think I'm being rude.')

'Yeah, I want to do a book,' he says with difficulty, his lower lip distended from the cancer treatment.

I tell him I want to find out what it was like being a little boy in Arnhem Land in the nineteen-fifties, his piece of the earth called Marwuyu Gulparil that is still an hour-and-a-half by four-wheel-drive and boat from already remote Ramingining.

I want to know about his mother. His father. His mob. About vacationing with Dennis Hopper at his New Mexico ranch after they became fast pals on *Mad Dog Morgan*, learning the mechanics of acting boozed courtesy of *Walkabout*'s John Meillon, his dinner with Bruce Lee in Rome, partying with Jimi

Hendrix and Bob Marley, about satisfying his hunger by killing one of the Queen's ducks at Buckingham Palace.

It's a very good story and came from a decent source. Is it true?

'Yeah, yeah,' he smiles in a manner that neither confirms nor denies the charge.

It isn't impossible.

Gulpilil's killings of a kangaroo and a goanna by spear and stick in *Walkabout* were so clean, so quick and painless, they didn't contravene the *Cinematograph Films (Animals) Act 1937*, which makes it illegal to 'distribute or exhibit material where the production involved inflicting pain or terror on an animal'.

Gulpilil likes his memories of meeting the Queen in 1971.

'Red carpet all the way from the plane to the car,' he says. 'Went looking around Buckingham Palace, then went to dinner, then went to see the Queen. Her Majesty! She opened it! Her Majesty the Queen opened it! Ffffffew!'

Gulpilil smacks his lips and picks at the skin on his fingers, which is peeling off because of the dryness of the air this far south.

He shows me a rock from Arnhem Land, a gift from Rolf de Heer during the filming of *Charlie's Country*.

'That's where I was born. Come from my country. A king brown snake.'

'There's a difference between the movie star and the man,' says Mary.

'And artist,' says Gulpilil.

— CHAPTER 3 —

My Brother Jack

SWINGING, SEXY-AS-A-BULL JACK THOMPSON, who is now seventy-eight and on a three-times-a-week dialysis program, cruises the Sydney harbourside car park in his 1985 Peugeot 505, which is navy blue and features a matching blue velour interior.

A sailing event has stolen all the available parking bays and I watch as the actor makes three circumnavigations of the car park, the familiar tile of golden hair visible above the door line as he circles the cafe we're meeting at.

When Thompson does stomp into view, still robust and with notes of the muscled shearer from *Sunday Too Far Away*, he pulls out his phone and shows a video message he'd sent to Gulpilil from the Kakadu set of *High Ground*, an Aboriginal resistance film, set in the nineteen-thirties, that Gulpilil was supposed to star in.

Thompson, who worked alongside Gulpilil in *Mad Dog Morgan* and *Australia*, has spent the last dozen years trying to get a film made about the various Indigenous wars in the new Australian colony.

First, it was going to be a film based on Eric Willmot's book, *Pemulwuy, the Rainbow Warrior*, about an Aboriginal fighter from Botany Bay whose guerrilla campaign struck terror into British settlers convinced he was impossible to kill.

As one colonist wrote, he had 'lodged in him, in shot, slugs and bullets about eight or ten ounces of lead, it is supposed he has killed over 30 of our people'.

When Pemulwuy was shot dead after fourteen years of resistance, the colony's Governor, Philip King, had his head preserved in spirits and shipped to the botanist Joseph Banks in London along with the note, 'A terrible pest to the colony, he was a brave and independent character'.

No one knows what happened to the grim relic.

It's a hell of a story.

'The first collective tale of Aboriginal resistance to the invasion,' says Thompson. 'You know, *of course there was* [resistance]! But we were brought up with a history that said they all got bad colds and died.'

Thompson says he was aware 'quite young that there was more to it than that. I was aware of the massacres'.

His connection with the Aboriginal world came early.

In 1946, Thompson's teacher at Narrabeen Primary in Sydney returned from a job on the set of the Chips Rafferty movie *Bush Christmas*, along with surprise guest Neza Saunders, the film's Aboriginal star, carrying boomerangs, singing tribal songs and demonstrating the formidable accuracy of his woomera–spear combo.

'After he left, the teachers had to stop all the boys from making spears,' he laughs.

Shortly after, Thompson's father, John, a feature writer and producer for ABC radio, went to East Arnhem Land for a National Geographic expedition.

The expedition's guide was the writer and former 'protector of Aborigines' Bill Harney, who'd married a part-Aboriginal woman in 1927, the first marriage of its sort to be officiated in the Northern Territory (Harney had to get permission from the 'Chief Protector of Aborigines' as part of the *Aboriginal*

Ordinance Act 1918, which regulated all aspects of Indigenous people's lives). Harney would later be the caretaker of what was then called Ayer's Rock.

To the joy of little Jack, his father returned home with sound recordings and eight-millimetre film. Harney's early books, *Taboo* (1943) and *Songs of the Songmen* (1949), gave the boy first-hand accounts of living with Australia's first people untainted by romantic notions of the noble savage or straight-up racism.

Harney's *Taboo*, which is a book of short stories, has an introduction by the anthropologist AP Elkin:

> From the moment he realized that the natives, though different from us, were human like ourselves, [Harney] has taken a sympathetic and intelligent interest in them, seeking to understand them ... almost every story in this book is a concrete illustration of the change wrought in the natives' manner of life by contact with the white man and his ways, and of the disastrous consequences.

In *Taboo*, stories included 'Reverie' where Harney ponders the similarities between white and black as he watches an old man singing Dreamtime songs to kids.

'Their numerous customs, so like our own, point to a common origin.'

In 'Justice', a man is brought up 'white' after his mother is chased off a cliff. In the town where he's been raised he, 'saw natives led about on chains, prisoners for some paltry offence, being given a feed of half-cooked rice and then a drink of water just before they got to town, so that, as they marched down the street, the people were amazed at the way they were treated – they looked so full. The knowing ones laughed at the joke – the police did well out of the native arrests, as they received one shilling a feed per man'.

The man responded by running away and beginning his own guerrilla war, 'carrying death to the white man in its trail' until he and his gang were killed.

'It fascinated me so much all I wanted to do was to go out... *there!*' says Thompson. 'For me it was, like, I don't have to go to Europe. I don't have to go to America. It's... *there!* It's on my doorstep. This. Extraordinary. Other. Thing.'

In the winter of 1955, and shortly before his fifteenth birthday, Harney helped Thompson get a job as a jackaroo on a cattle station a couple of hundred clicks northwest of Alice Springs on the Elkedra River.

'Mate, I was gone forever once that happened,' says Thompson. 'I was the only white fella there and all the Alyawarre men [whose tribal land in Central Australia extends over forty-six thousand square kilometres] spoke their language and treated me like their son.'

In what way?

'They looked after me. They didn't *baby me*. They treated me like a young man.'

When Thompson arrived, the station owner told him, 'There's no work here for boys.'

'And I was colourblind, mate,' says Thompson. 'I was with these wonderful people, men who knew so much more than me about what we were *supposed to be doing*. You know, mustering cattle over one thousand five hundred square miles of unfenced territory, unmarked, no roads. And they treated me with great respect and affection and they set out to teach me about just simple things, knowing which *direction* things were in, where you are, and all of that. And they continued their ritual life.'

Thompson recalls a group of young men being brought into the camp for their tribal initiation because three significant elders essential to the rites were working there.

'They did the big initiation song and dance there and I was lying down on my swag and my eyes were... *wide... open*. After that happened, it very much became a part of me,' says Thompson. 'It was wonderful moment for me. They taught me just by being who they are, living the way they live, they taught me for the rest of my life, that I belong here.'

Thompson stares at me. One white fella to another.

'We don't feel that. We talk about man versus nature. We talk about overcoming. We see ourselves as dealing with it. They know they are... *it*. And like every other creature, they belong here. They belong here.'

Thompson cocks his head. He pauses, in his theatrical way.

'That's a big thing to be taught at fifteen.'

It wasn't the only great life lesson.

One day, Thompson was in the station's ute as it came up on the Aboriginal camp where he went every day to count the goats that had been milked. In 1955, it was goat's milk or nothing because of a recent hit of bovine tuberculosis.

The white driver looked at Thompson and, without any particular malice, said, 'Look at them. All they do is eat, fuck and sleep.'

Thompson's eyes widened.

'They *do*?'

'And I wondered, how do I get that job? I learned something there. Never mind ambition, *that'll do!*'

Oh, reader, if you could hear the laughter of the great actor. It kickstarts from an intermittent rumble to a propeller roaring at full revolution, like the seaplanes a few hundred metres across the harbour on their summer joy flights.

Thompson quietens and returns to his Pemulwuy movie. These wars, called 'frontier' and 'pastoral' wars, and which extended from first settlement in 1788 and into the nineteen-thirties, weren't as one-sided as you might think.

'The fact that these happened needs to be told,' says Thompson. 'It needs to be a part of our history. It's who we are. Our children need to know that. All of us need to know this.'

In his book, *The Sydney Wars, Conflict in the Early Colony 1788–1817*, Stephen Gapps writes of the accepted, but flawed, narrative of Europeans overwhelming Aboriginal people with modern weaponry.

> Early colonists – both military and civilian – recognised violent confrontation around Sydney as part of ongoing warfare, and many wrote about it as war. Both sides adapted their weapons and tactics in response to those of the opposition. The British conducted numerous difficult campaigns against combatants who held the distinct advantages of terrain and local knowledge. Aboriginal warriors won several battles and often stretched the limits of the colonial military forces.

Pemulwuy, the film, didn't get made.

Turning Willmot's book, which Thompson describes as a novel based on historical truths, into a movie was too complex and would've required the extended canvas of a television series.

Eventually, he was directed to *Man Tracks*, written in 1937 by the prolific Australian author Ion 'Jack' Idriess, whose books sold upwards of three million copies during the Great Depression.

'It was about the mounted police patrols of the nineteen-twenties and into the nineteen-thirties, in the Top End there. The black rebellion,' says Thompson. 'About this band of guys burning down cattle stations, stealing cattle, deliberately trying to prevent the settling of that area by white pastoralists. And, it's wonderful stuff, but there's also a woman who led a band of raiders and scared the shit out of everyone. Black Mary! And she worried the black guys too!'

For *High Ground*, elements of *Man Tracks* have been blended with a story about an Aboriginal boy who survives a massacre and is taken to a mission as a baby. When he grows up he's ordered by patrol officers to track down a man who turns out to be his grandfather.

'And that,' growls Thompson, 'is when we get into trouble!'

Don't tell me any more, I beg. Who needs a plot spoiler?

'But that's what we're doing! And Gulparil [As Jack prefers to call his old friend, an abbreviation of Marwuyu Gulparil, where Gulpilil was born] was going to be in it, right up to the last minute. Had we done it last year he might still have been able to do it. I kept on checking with him and Mary right until the last minute. But in the end he couldn't do it.'

There is a cosmic synchronicity, however.

'When he was declared to be . . . ah . . .'

Thompson ponders the most delicate way to say terminally ill or dying.

'. . . on his last legs . . .'

Thompson strikes an ain't-no-way-to-sugarcoat-a-death-sentence face.

'. . . he asked me, would I get in touch with [former Yothu Yindi singer] Witiyana Marika, who is the man who, in Yolngu cultural terms, will sing David into the next world. So he's the man! You know, in that complex system of relationships that the Aboriginal people have, he's related as an uncle figure and a senior culture man.'

'It's a wonderful piece of irony, and that's the way it's meant to be. The man who will be responsible for David's passage into the next life ends up playing the last role that David would've played.'

Thompson breaks into an Aboriginal accent and addresses his old friend: 'Witiyana did a good job but he didn't do a Gulparil, ay.'

Almost fifty years earlier, when the teenage Gulpilil was lighting up screens across the world in *Walkabout*, Thompson was a thirty-year-old thespian on the make.

He knew, when he saw *Walkabout*, that there had been a profound cultural shift.

In the documentary, *Gulpilil: One Red Blood* (2002), Thompson says it 'was the first time I'd seen the Aboriginal culture presented on screen as not only interesting but *dynamically attractive*! And *sexy*! The guy was sexy! No Australian director would've done that. It would have not until then been culturally possible for us to think of an Aboriginal young man as being sexually attractive to a Western woman'.

Today, he says, 'For a lot of people, in Australia, that was truly shocking. Because there's no doubt he's a good-looking fella. The girls will tell you that. It was quite a revolution.'

Five years after *Walkabout*, Thompson and Gulpilil became fast pals while shooting *Mad Dog Morgan* in rural Victoria.

'It was ... *there* ... that I developed a respect for David as a practitioner of my craft, as an actor, as an actor for film. There was always, in David, an extraordinary level of performance that was there in his tribal dance, but he learned [to act] as a young man on *Walkabout* and when he arrived to do *Mad Dog Morgan* he knew *exactly* what was needed in front of the camera. He has an extraordinary presence, whatever that word means. It's very real. Some people have it and some people don't. And David has it, but he also knows how to feed the camera. That's a phrase Donald Pleasence gave to me on my first feature film, *Wake in Fright*.'

Thompson says that he and the film's lead, Gary Bond, were talking about the difference between acting for stage and acting for screen, and Pleasence, who plays the crazy alcoholic ex-doctor, Doc Tydon, walked up behind him and whispered, 'Feed the camera, Jack'.

It was a lesson that stuck.

'And David *knows that*. He *knows* that,' says Thompson. 'When I saw him in *Mad Dog Morgan* I knew that he was aware of that. It was such a joy to see him at work.'

Thompson says he and Gulpilil bonded over the non-verbal signals that he'd learned to recognise when he was a teenage jackaroo.

'There was an immediate open door. We were immediately brothers. Because I was exposed to it at age fifteen, it was just so familiar to me. So when David started doing that stuff, I went, yeah, it's so clear and so specific. It's not exactly telepathy, but there's a lot of non-verbal communication. It's a natural part of the Aboriginal world, that ancient old tradition.'

Thompson's face twists into various forms.

'That's kangaroo. That's emu.'

He twists his mouth left then right then back again.

'It's this wonderful sign language. Dat way. *Dat way*. That fella. *That fella*.'

Like *Mad Dog Morgan*'s director Philippe Mora, whom we'll discover shortly, Thompson recalls the racism rife in Australia in the mid-seventies, and that was directed at Gulpilil in the small towns of Victoria.

'Country towns, *if* they served Aboriginal people at all at a pub and sold them booze, it was at a window around the back somewhere. They were never allowed in the bar,' says Thompson. 'For so long, they were not even citizens. They were not even considered to be human. They were part of the fauna of this country. And, so, it was not just an attitude of they're ... lesser ... it was a truly prejudicial attitude. *Bloody blacks*. And I know that it comes from guilt. I'm old enough to remember World War II and what it was like. World War II, the blacks, the Japs and the Germans, they're all fucking monsters, they eat babies ... '

Thompson's voice drops to a whisper. He leans forward. We meet in the middle, he for effect, me to catch his words.

'It seems to be a part of warfare that you attach that quality to the people you kill. It justifies you killing them. And in some way, we've done that in this country with the Aboriginal people and we haven't gotten around to admitting it. So there's a rejection of them in a very deep and vile way. And there's nothing more Aboriginal than Gulpilil. He walks into the bar and he's not a *part*-Aboriginal person, so that's *war*. It was a red flag to those guys.'

Thompson says the bartender looked at Gulpilil and said, 'Nope! We don't serve you people in there!'

'Well,' Thompson told him. 'If you don't serve him, you don't serve us.'

Gulpilil had seen it before. He lived it every day.

'For him it was ordinary,' says Thompson. 'For a lot of us, it was truly shocking because we don't live with a lot of Aboriginal people in Sydney. You can live most of your life in Sydney and not see Aboriginal people. It's only because of the life I lived that I do have something to do with them.'

I ask Thompson how he feels stardom affected a tribal kid taken off a mission in Arnhem Land and tossed into a world where every wish is granted, ego fed, and all in a foreign language.

'David was walking a cultural tightrope, half in the white world where he was bringing the black world to the white world and half in the black world bringing his experiences in the white world. I haven't seen too many of us from our culture who could handle that.'

How has Gulpilil coped?

'At times it's been incredibly disturbing to him. In our world, the world of ... *show biz* ... every second or third night it's a party. It's the actor's disease. Too much drinking at the end of a play or show. You're wound up, you're high on the performance itself and you sit around and you celebrate. And at times it did bring David undone.'

The important caveat here, says Thompson, is 'at times'.

'It didn't bring him down. And it is his monumental courage and stamina that has taken him there.'

Beyond *Mad Dog*, Thompson and Gulpilil shared the same theatrical agent, John Cann, who created a trust fund for Gulpilil's sporadic earnings.

'David received a lot of money and then nothing. For months and months and months. And then a whole lot of money. It is a part of the Indigenous culture that if I come back with a kangaroo, then we all eat it. It's communal and it's particularly communal with family. So when David would come back with a whole lot of money . . .' Thompson breaks into accent, '"*Hey David! Wouldn't mind a Toyota!*"

'And, in a sense, he's culturally obliged to buy it. So, when David was out of money, he'd call John and say, "I'm out of money," and John'd say, "Well, I gave it all to you. It's all gone now, what are we going to do?"

'So John established a trust that made certain that the money wasn't all taken at once.'

The pair also shared the same manager in America, Michael McLean.

'David came around to Michael's place in LA a couple of times. One time, David was there with John [Cann], myself, my wife, and we were going back to Australia and a car had been called to pick us up. The car turned up and David was in full flight. He came out and danced and sang at that car . . .'

Thompson mimics Gulpilil's dance, arms out, eyes flared.

'Michael came out and he asked the driver, "Are you okay?" And the guy said, "This is great! God, this is like Discovery! It's like being on the Discovery Channel." The driver had found himself in the middle of this wonderful moment. There's this vitality in David, this wonderful life stream that's there, right from the go. In *Walkabout* you see it. You see it in that young, slightly reticent young man, this vitality. It's extraordinary that it's always been there.'

Thompson stops. He's enveloped in nostalgia, love.

'We missed you on the movie, mate.'

He stops again.

'He is my brother. He is my brother. I feel for him right now. I was thinking about him last night because it was the Actor Awards and they had photographs up on the wall and there was David accepting his award and there was David and I up on the wall. He's up there with the best actors. And he opened that door for us [to the Aboriginal world]. There was an attempt with *Jedda* to open that door for us, showing this extraordinary cultural connection, but it was shown as it was viewed at the time, as something separate and closed off because of its relationship between two Aboriginal people, an Aboriginal man and an Aboriginal woman. There are elements of it there, but there's not that overt expression of that cultural identity that's *there* in the young David in *Walkabout*. There in the dance, there in the capacity to...' Thompson winds up, like a baseball pitcher about to throw a fast ball. '... *he lives there! I belong here!*

'That fabulous contrast in that picture of these totally lost, disassociated white people in this land in which he lives so easily and enthusiastically. That's the doorway to sixty thousand years of continuous tradition, the oldest in the world. Through David we can learn from the values and vitality of the oldest continual cultural continuum on the planet. That he is a part of. And that he brings into our world. He is a gateway to a history that we've so far denied and not embraced. He deserves, well he is honoured, but he deserves to be recognised. He's an extraordinary figure. In this country, he's more important than Ned Kelly.'

I ask, in your heart and your head, what do you think about when I say David Gulpilil? Thompson's eyes glaze, then drip.

If they were the windscreen of his Peugeot 505, the old wipers would be struggling to clear the sudden cloudburst.

'I think of him as my brother. I think of him with great affection, love. I think of David with love. I feel *for* him, and he *was* a hero. And I love him dearly.'

— CHAPTER 4 —

Gulpilil vs Dennis Hopper

IN THE SPRING AND EARLY SUMMER OF 1975, GULPILIL starred alongside counter-culture icon Dennis Hopper in the Ozploitation classic *Mad Dog Morgan*, a film its director describes as 'setting grotesque 19th-century human behaviour against an extraordinary landscape'.

As was the fashion of Australian directors in the seventies, Philippe Mora portrays the bushranger Morgan as a victim of cruel colonial justice, a Robin Hood character driven to crime after witnessing a massacre of Chinese labourers in the Riverina goldfields.

A story in the Victorian newspaper *The Singleton Argus*, which appeared in 1924 and was headlined 'BLOODTHIRSTY MORGAN', has a different take. It describes Morgan as 'the high priest of infamy. Morgan was a monster rather than a man, his lust for blood was insatiable, and he tortured his victims for the pleasure their writhings gave him'.

Early in the film, Hopper is gang-raped in prison. And after being killed in the film's climactic scene, his corpse is decapitated and the scrotal sac removed so Police Superintendent Cobham, played by Frank Thring with his trademark withering wickedness, might have a unique tobacco pouch.

'I wasn't trying to be controversial or provocative, I was just trying to be factual,' says Mora, now seventy and living in the shadow of West Hollywood's Chateau Marmont Hotel in Los Angeles. 'There were plenty of horror stories going on in Australia at that time. You didn't need to exaggerate if you stuck to the facts.'

Did the gay gang-bang scene cause trouble with your masters, the Australian Film Commission, who were funded by the federal government?

'Well,' says Mora, 'what you're calling the... uh... gay... uh... bang... gang... that caused *a lot* of trouble. But, you know, it's usually women getting attacked in movies, not men. The head of the Australian Film Commission was mortified and he said to me after the screening, "Listen Philippe, we're getting money from the federal government to promote tourism and a Hollywood star getting buggered is not going to help tourism in Australia!" And, being a bit of a smart arse, I said, well, I disagree with you. I think it'll *help* tourism.'

Side note: Tourism to Australia did increase in the year following *Mad Dog Morgan*'s release, although Mora concedes the uptick in visitors had nothing to do with Hopper's on-screen travails.

Hopper was almost forty and had already starred in a raft of Hollywood blockbusters, including *Giant, Rebel Without a Cause, Cool Hand Luke* and the zeitgeist-shifting *Easy Rider*, made for 400k and grossing sixty mill, and which Hopper credited with popularising cocaine in the US.

'The cocaine problem in the United States is really because of me. There was no cocaine on the street before *Easy Rider*. After *Easy Rider*, it was everywhere,' said Hopper.

In its 2010 obituary after Hopper had died, aged seventy-four of prostate cancer, *Rolling Stone* magazine described him as 'one of Hollywood's most notorious drug addicts'.

One morning on the shoot, Mora was woken up by yodelling. He found Hopper in his room, surrounded by members of the crew, drinking Old Spice aftershave.

'We ran out of beer,' said a crew member.

'Not having seen anyone consume this amount of alcohol and assorted drugs, I convinced myself that Hopper would die before completion and shipwreck my career. Although I could not deny the powerful on-screen result, I truly thought the bastard was going to destroy me,' Mora wrote in 2010.

Gulpilil was twenty-two and living in Arnhem Land after his turn in *Walkabout* before being written into *Mad Dog* by Mora. He would be given third billing on the film, behind Hopper and Jack Thompson, who was fresh off the hit film *Sunday Too Far Away*.

Gulpilil found Hopper, who stayed in character and was, according to Mora, 'inflamed by Stanislavski, rum, beer and psychedelics', an impossible cultural bridge to cross.

'It was a complex movie to make because of Dennis and how he was and his background and his training. He didn't understand David at the beginning and David didn't understand him,' says Mora.

Two weeks into filming, Gulpilil told Mora that he was going to take a ten-minute break; he disappeared into the bush.

Ten minutes turned into one day.

'It was a disaster for the movie,' says Mora. 'I didn't know there was a problem. David didn't come to me and nor did Dennis. I don't think any of us knew there was problem. David was keeping it to himself and then he finally thought, "Fuck it, I'm taking off".'

Mora called the police.

'And they told me, "We don't know how to find him, he's gone walkabout". They said I'd have to get Aboriginal trackers to find him,' says Mora. 'So these two fantastic old Aboriginal trackers with white beards came in to see me. They went into David's motel room and they were smelling things, lifting things up, collecting things. And after an hour, they came up to me and said, "Okay mate, we'll go find David for you!"

'And, they disappeared into the bush. Four hours later they came back with David. I had *no* idea how they found him. It was unbelievable. The area we were in, now it's more developed, but when we made the film it was hardcore bush. Anyway, they found him and I said, "David, you can't just walk off in the middle of the movie."

Gulpilil said he left because he needed to ask the kookaburras and the trees about Hopper.

Mora asked Gulpilil for the fauna's assessment.

'They said that he's crazy,' Gulpilil told the director.

'I could've told you that,' said Mora, who begged, 'Please don't go walkabout again.'

Thirty years later in his one-man show, Gulpilil would explain, 'When you workin' with people like Mr Hopper and Mr John Meillon well . . . you gonna learn about drinkin' and drugs. And it was the nineteen-seventies. And I thought: "Well . . . I gotta join in. This is white fella's corroboree." And you gotta be part of it. I tell you what though . . . I never seen nothin' like it before. If a young white fella was goin' through all this . . . well it would probably do his head in. So imagine what it was like for a young black fella from the top of Australia who'd never left the bush! Fuck me swingin' sideways!'

On set, Hopper was 'mortified' he'd offended his co-star.

Says Mora: 'When he heard the story he went *out of his way* to be friendly and to make David feel comfortable and to talk about the culture clash, the American movie star from Hollywood meets David Gulpilil from the Northern Territory. He was so concerned about it all that he asked David to stay with him in the motel. And, you know, Dennis *was* Mad Dog so he said to David, "Look, in the story, we live together, so let's stay in the same room and see how that goes." It was a way of

Dennis explaining their relationship, a kind of method acting. I found that very sweet and their relationship was very sweet. And, then, in the movie, Dennis puts his arm around him at one point and says, "I love you, man." At a screening at the Montreal Film Festival, there was a Q and A for me and the first question was, "Is Mad Dog Morgan . . . *gay*?" I said, "What are you talking about?" "Well, there's that scene where he puts his arm around him . . ." I had to explain, "No, no, no, they're just good friends."'

Different times.

Back when racism came to a man's lips as casually as a post-dinner cigarette in a restaurant. Here, Mora's version of the episode told earlier by Jack Thompson.

'David came in with the crew and such was those times in Australia that the guy who owned the bar said he wouldn't serve a black! Dennis was enraged! And they all started to walk out and the barman said, "It's okay, mate, I'm sorry, I apologise." That was Dennis's civil-rights training. He actually marched with Martin Luther King. He'd been in that situation in the American south and so, you know, he struck a blow there for the Aboriginals in that area.'

As for Gulpilil, 'He was very happy because he couldn't believe it when everyone said, if you don't serve him, you don't serve us.'

French-born Mora is the son of European Jews, the noted artist Mirka Mora and her husband, the restaurateur and gallery owner Georges. He says the first Aboriginal he ever saw was the painter Albert Namatjira. It was 1954, he remembers, because it was also the year the Queen visited Australia for the first time.

'I grew up in an aggressively non-prejudiced family so [racism] was never an issue, but seeing Namatjira did make a deep impression on me,' he says. 'He was this awesome-looking guy and he came to my home because my parents had an exhibition of the modern artists at the time, like Charles Blackman, the Boyds, John Perceval and people that are all iconic now. There had been an article in a newspaper and Namatjira came to see the paintings accompanied by two detectives! Aboriginals weren't even allowed to walk around by themselves! Absolutely amazing! It was at the time of the incredibly named White Australia policy. It's hard to believe now. It was sad. The only Aboriginal I had seen until I met him in our home was on stamps! So I really enjoyed that aspect of *Mad Dog Morgan*, positioning David within an Australian historical story. And it was a big deal to have an Indigenous man as a co-lead.'

How was Gulpilil to direct?

'Well, look, he's a director's dream 'cause I didn't have to direct him. He just knew what to do. He was just a pleasure and I've never met an actor quite that... natural...'

Mora thinks about his paltry description.

Natural?

'No, natural is too small a word for it. He didn't have to do much to get your attention because he was so charismatic. And that smile! That smile could burn houses down! He is always a standout, a standout.'

There's the usual caveats.

When I ask Mora what sort of direction he'd give Gulpilil, he goes quiet, lets the air out of the tyres... *phhhhhhhoooooo*... and says, 'That's a... *big*... question.'

'Listen,' he says, 'I saw Orson Welles at a dinner years ago, he was promoting one of his movies and he was the after-dinner speaker. Someone asked him what a director did and he replied that a director is someone who presides over accidents.'

Margaret Carnegie, writer-historian and patron of the arts, who along with Mora's father Georges funded the film, lived in Holbrook and had spent twelve years researching and writing a scholarly tome called *Morgan: The Bold Bushranger*, which Mora employed as an ongoing encyclopedia.

Carnegie, who would campaign for a treaty with Indigenous Australians during the country's bicentenary in 1988 and who would be adopted as a full sister of the tribal elder and artist Nelson (Nosepeg) Tjupurrula, also had a fine collection of Indigenous artefacts and paintings.

Carnegie asked Mora if Gulpilil might have an interest in examining the collection.

'Of course he did,' says Mora. 'It was a huge collection. [But] he freaked out, really. He was looking at stuff that not only white people weren't supposed to see but ... *he* ... wasn't supposed to see. Secret artefacts and sacred artefacts from other tribes from all over Australia. It must've blown his mind. He grabbed this really big boomerang, a killing boomerang, and she said, "Oh my god, David, please be careful with that!" It was from 1820 or something. David pulled out this big knife and said, "Don't worry, I'm going to fix it!" and he started carving bits off! And Margaret, god bless her, at first she started freaking out, but then, she said, "Okay, David, go ahead, go ahead."'

After the shoot, Gulpilil strolled a few red carpets, did some interviews, became pally with Frank Thring and took up Hopper's invitation to stay at his New Mexico ranch, Hopper having been forced to leave Australia quicker than he might've imagined.

According to Mora, 'When we finished shooting *Mad Dog Morgan*, he rode off in costume, poured a bottle of O.P. rum into the real Morgan's grave in front of my mother Mirka Mora, drank one himself, got arrested and deported the next day, with a blood-alcohol reading that said he should have been clinically dead, according to the judge studying his alcohol tests.'

Mora, meanwhile, says he saw Gulpilil over the years, but lost contact when he moved to LA for work.

'I always loved the guy,' he says. 'But different worlds. He had his problems, unfortunately. He's a phenomenon to've survived living in both worlds. He must have an amazing mind. I don't think it's been easy.'

—— CHAPTER 5 ——

The Queers on the Hill

Fifteen minutes out of Murray Bridge, and heading towards Tailem Bend, is Lauriston Park, which offers 'breaking and training services, young stock prep and showing and clipping services' for horses. Proprietors: Michael Higginbottom and Terry Hocking.

Terry is Gulpilil's best friend in town, the man who presented him with his ornate walking cane, which I'd admired on my first visit. Before Terry's gift, Gulpilil used a stick that had been previously occupied jamming shut the windows of his and Mary's little rental at night.

I arrive at Lauriston Park on a dark winter's night, approaching the yellow-brick farmhouse with its green gabled roof via a U-shaped driveway. No lights are visible. The winter moon illuminates two colonial-style chairs, painted white, which are empty on the porch. A horse, with a blanket on its back, shuffles back and forth in the front paddock.

Dogs bark.

I imagine abrupt country folk and edgy farm dogs with liver-mush breath.

I bang on a screen door.

Surprise.

A tall man dances down the hallway, swings open the door and reveals . . . oh, reader, if you'll look right over my shoulder it's a little piece of Buckingham Palace on the Murray! Walls painted mint-green, beautifully restored antique cupboards and tables and chairs, with framed paintings and photos on the wall. Lamps spray a delicate warm light upon the walls and the fine upholstered lounge chairs.

'Hellllllloooo!'

This ain't *Wake in Fright*.

Terry is revealed to be an urbane gay man married to Lauriston Park's other proprietor, Michael Higginbottom, whose day job is as support crew to various disabled people in the area.

Terry is a chef by trade and a horse prepper and clipper by love. Terry met Gulpilil three years ago when he was a chef at the Swanport Hotel just out of Murray Bridge. Turn right at Swanport Road and you can't miss it.

Terry had arrived from Adelaide the previous year, fulfilling a dream to have thirty acres, an impossible ask in the city, and Gulpilil was new to the joint too, when Darwin became impossible to bear.

One day, Mary brought Gulpilil into the Swanport and asked Terry if it was possible to whip up a barramundi and chips. If he can't physically be in Arnhem Land, at least give the man a taste of home. Soon, Mary and Gulpilil were eating lunch and dinner there every day.

When they're not working, Terry and Michael are crisscrossing the country with their horses. Terry estimates he and Michael will smash twenty thousand kilometres a year in their Hino truck, the horse floats attached via hitch. At the shows, Michael rides and Terry handles the horses.

Often the pair will stop for a relaxing port midway through a journey at some favoured regional hotel, but, mostly, it's music on, hands on the wheel, let's eat up the bitumen.

On the night I arrive, Terry has been to Horsham, in Victoria, and back. Left at dawn, got back at five. Eight hundred clicks.

'We're at the top of our game now,' says Terry, after the successful show.

I tell Terry, and Michael, white shirt, blue jeans, an immaculate figure, who has just entered the scene, that their appearance surprised me. More than surprised, I say.

I was relieved.

I came expecting farmers in filthy overalls, boots that could kick hell out of man or animal, pigskin hats decorated with bullets, and tobacco being spat on the ground.

'We're the *gay* farmers!' says Michael.

'We're the queers on the hill!' says Terry.

'The housewives of Monteith,' says Michael.

'Some of the shit we do, I tell you,' says Terry.

Skinny dipping in the Murray River is a favourite.

'Drunk as skunks. We fucking love it,' says Terry.

In the backyard, a red male mannequin has been outfitted in a knee-length dress. Normally it has a bobbed blonde wig as per Marilyn Monroe.

'She lost her fucking wig again. The dogs probably fucking took off with it,' says Michael.

'Got it from a friend who owns Cherry Lane,' says Terry. 'I want a gold one, I want them all through the garden.'

Every day, Gulpilil will call Terry and ask him where he's cooking 'cause Tez now cooks at a few joints in the area after he quit his job at the Swanport. If it's too far away, he'll tell Gulpilil he's not working just so Mary doesn't have to pilot their little Hyundai all over the place.

The friendship has blossomed.

Gulpilil ate everywhere Terry cooked, then started coming to their house every day. He sits in one of the stuffed armchairs and asks for the heater to be cranked up, even if it's thirty degrees outside.

Together, Terry and Gulpilil will watch his old movies. Gulpilil signs his DVDs with a special gold Texta.

'I'm very lucky to have them,' says Terry.

A favourite film of both men is *Charlie's Country*.

'I cry every time in that,' says Terry.

Whenever the scene comes up where Gulpilil and his pal Black Pete (Peter Djigirr) steal a car, only to run out of fuel, Terry will tell Gulpilil he's a 'fucking idiot!'

Terry laughs, sighs, laughs again.

'I say, why did you pinch that car? It hardly had any fucking petrol in it! For god's sake, David! You ... *dickheads!*'

His favourite memory of their three-year friendship is the sixty-fifth birthday party he threw for Gulpilil, in July 2018.

'I wanted something unique for David. I thought, "What's David?" He's a bushman. He's lived out in the middle of nowhere and lived on nothing. So what I decided to do was to have a huge bonfire, a massive bonfire. I called it *David's House Without a Roof*. We had a lounge room set up and another sitting room near another fire ... all outside. We had a table that could sit sixty people under a big marquee. And then we had a bedroom set up with all the side lamps and you name it. His family came and we had a long dinner. We had all sorts of meat: turkey, lamb, chicken, beef, pork. We didn't have fish because he said, "Nope, don't want fish, I want to try all these different meats." We had speeches, lots of carry-on. It was a full-on night for David.'

When the party ran out of wood for the fire, Terry announced they'd be burning the furniture.

'We burned lounge after lounge after lounge. We thought, we'll stay warm and it's only furniture, so let's just keep burning it. And everybody was going, "Oh my god, Terry, you are burning this furniture." David was in awe. And I said, "Well, David, what would you do in the bush if you were cold?"'

Gulpilil laughed and said he'd set a car on fire.

Later, Gulpilil told Terry he'd never had a birthday party before, at least on this scale, and told him how much it meant to him.

'He got here at three o'clock when the sun was still up. I asked him if he wanted to lie down, to have a rest before the party, and he said, "No, no, no, I'm not going to miss a minute."'

When Gulpilil asked him if it was possible to organise a party for his sixty-sixth, Terry told him, of course, 'You can have four a year if you want!'

Together they eat, they sing, Gulpilil tells stories.

'Culturally, I've learned a lot of different things. David, being a sick man, when he uses the tissues you can't burn the tissues. You have to actually dispose of them in the bin or, even better, down the toilet. If you had the fire on, and an elder like David used a tissue, you'd never grab it off the table and throw it on the fire. I think he'd flatten ya! You can't burn anything out of him.'

Gulpilil told him of his plans when he dies.

'He gets very emotional about what he wants. He's spoken to me in-depth about taking his body back home. It's really sad, but it's something he wants to talk about. He said, "You will throw the earth on me. You are going to be right next to me when they put me down the hole." I said, "That's up to your family", and he said, "No, I'm the elder!" He's really, really strong about it. I'm very emotional about it because I love the man. He's been here, a solid three years, with me. In that three years, a day hasn't gone by where I haven't seen him. It will rock my world when he dies.'

Can he explain the connection?

'I'm an idiot. I speak the truth. It's my way or the highway. Just like David. Look at his life in Darwin. He said, "The law is the law and I don't believe in it. Fuck you." I'm the same. I am blessed that David has come into our lives and accepted us as who we are, Michael and I being partners, he has accepted all that, he accepts everybody in life.'

Three months ago, and just before Terry flew over to Perth for a horse show, Gulpilil called. Said he didn't think he was going to make it. Could he come and say goodbye?

'He said, "Brother, I don't think I'll see you again. I know you gotta go, but come down and see me." I spent two nights in a row with him at the hospital. His dream is to get better and take me back to Gulparil. He says, "I'm going to make you swim with crocodile!" Oh my god, oh, I don't ... want ... to ... swim ... with ... crocodiles. He tells me he'll look after me. He tells me everything about the crocodile and he says, "I will save you, I will save you!"'

Does he think it'll happen?

'I really don't know. I wish it would. That would be a dream I'd never forget.'

Right now, 4 October 2018, Gulpilil wants, more than anything, to see another Christmas. Until he met Terry he'd never had a traditional Christmas lunch and dinner combo, something Terry excels at, and thrives on – the setting up, the preparation, the inevitable drama, the treasure, the trash. Terry will cut boxthorns out of the garden, spray 'em white and make Christmas trees.

'David will come in November and we'll start decorating the house. It's all very English. It's got a lot of decorations, traditional decorations. At Christmas, oh god, he's like a kid in a candy shop. He's here at the crack of dawn, then he'll snooze a bit, get back into the tucker, go home for a little bit, come back, he's just full on! I'll say, "Oh David, slow down! Fuck!"'

Terry's smile disappears.

'We've got to keep the dream alive for him. We've got to do as much as we can with what life he has left. We've got to keep him looking forward to ... *something*.'

CHAPTER 6

Gulpilil Wins the Archibald

A MAN WITH THE ROPING BODY OF A BOXER enters the inner-city Sydney bar arm in arm with an elegant Peruvian to discuss his 2004 Archibald prize–winning portrait of Gulpilil, *Two Worlds*.
The artist is Craig Ruddy, whom you'll know if you travel in fashionable artistic circles, but who was an unknown in 2004 when his mixed-media interpretation of Gulpilil swept the Archy.

Main prize. People's Choice. The media couldn't get enough of the 204 × 240-centimetre work, which came in four pieces and had to be bolted together, and that was entered with roughly five minutes left.

Wasn't this why the Archibald existed? To celebrate the uniqueness of Australian culture and bright new talent?

It depended who you spoke to.

Trouble was already brewing.

Ruddy's fifty now; looks thirty. He wears a fitted T-shirt, jeans, boots and slouchy baker boy cap. A rabbit grin, scarecrow hair and large spectacles complete a favourable tableau of The Artist. The Peruvian man, whose tropical shirt is opened to reveal the hairless, reddish brown-coloured skin of his Indigenous DNA, is the actor Roberto Meza, Ruddy's partner of eighteen years, and who played Geoffrey Rush's rented lover in the movie *Candy*.

'This is Jorge,' says Rush in that 2006 movie, as Meza reclines on the bed, his little red shorts dangerously inflated. 'Very limited English but a *very large* penis.'

Ruddy and Meza live in a country town called The Pocket, out behind Byron Bay on the New South Wales North Coast, with a sprawling studio and minimalist low-slung house. In 2004, Meza was sowing various oats abroad while Ruddy pursued his art dream in Sydney.

It had been only two years since Ruddy had made the decision, encouraged by Meza, to become a full-time artist, telling Ruddy to increase his credit card limit from $2000 to $10,000.

Buy your freedom. Make it work.

On a whim in 2003, Ruddy entered a self-portrait into the Archibald.

'It got a lot of attention, I loved it, they invited me to do a presentation and a talk and I thought, "Oh wow, I want to do this seriously next year,"' says Ruddy. 'And the number one person I wanted to celebrate was David Gulpilil. I remembered him from *Walkabout* and *Storm Boy*. He was a hero for me.'

Ruddy grew up in Forestville on Sydney's northern beaches, a suburb that butts up against the Garigal National Park.

'I grew up in that park. I spent my life in the bush so I had a really deep and strong connection with the environment and the land. I always fantasised about living with the Indigenous culture,' he says. 'In my mind, that was the ultimate way to live, to be fully connected and integrated in harmony with the environment. It was the way I wanted to live. I didn't like the whole idea of the Western world and the Western culture and the way we lived in the cities. Gulpilil was inspirational. He was what I aspired to.'

Ruddy wanted to create Gulpilil's portrait on English colonial wallpaper, the juxtaposition of the Indigenous man empowered over the culture that caused the ongoing Aboriginal catastrophe.

At first, he was thinking of a Florence Broadhurst design, but when he went to the man who owned the rights, David Lennie of Signature Prints, Lennie loved the idea so much he ushered Ruddy into the storeroom, an Aladdin's Cave of wallpaper.

'Grab whatever you need,' he told the artist.

Ruddy walked out with various offcuts and an almost-finished roll. Lennie pulled him aside and said, 'Do you realise what you've got there? That's the wallpaper that lines the wall of the dining room of Admiralty House [the Sydney home of Australia's governor-general].'

'So it was perfect,' says Ruddy. 'Bringing Indigenous culture to the dining table of Admiralty House. That's ... *exactly* ... what I wanted.'

Ruddy used every piece of wallpaper on that roll, cutting it and pasting it to the four boards that would make up the canvas for *Two Worlds*.

And then it sat there. For over three months.

Finding David Gulpilil wasn't, still isn't, easy.

'It got to the point where I thought, this isn't going to happen and I'd given up on the idea. So I went travelling down south with a few Spanish friends but when I came back I met up with an artist friend, Yosi. We were having lunch and he told me about the events that had taken place that weekend. While I was away, a young Indigenous boy on his pushbike had been chased by police through Redfern. He rode through a wire fence and died horrifically, sparking major riots. It got me so revved up and angry that I called David's agent and left a message stating, "I'm coming to your office and I'm not leaving until I get to speak to you."'

Just before Ruddy arrived at the office the agent called back, told him he liked the concept, and that he'd throw it in front of his client.

Gulpilil loved the idea. But rehearsals for his one-man show, which was to premiere at the Adelaide Festival, weren't exactly working, and they were planning on cancelling it.

The agent told Ruddy, 'Call this number tomorrow at eight in the morning and if they're cancelling the show you can get in to see David because he'll be staying for the weekend before flying back to Ramingining.'

It was two weeks before the deadline for the Archibald. Ruddy called. He was told the show was going to be cancelled and to 'get in and get out'.

'David was out the back of Windsor [in Sydney's northwest], on a remote property in the bush so, you know, I got these crazy directions: at the third large tree turn left. When you see a large jagged rock, turn right and go down the hill. I ended up there the next morning about 9 am and the funny thing was that I had a Spanish mate staying with me at the time, Agustin, a bit of a party boy and a professional hockey player, and he was coming to help me because the boards were . . . *big*. It was in four pieces so I could get it in the van but then I had to screw it together when I got there.'

Even though the show was set to be cancelled, rehearsals continued. Ruddy turned up and was told to wait twenty minutes and then he'd have Gulpilil's attention for one hour.

'When we arrived on the set it was all really heavy. It was not a good vibe at all. Things didn't feel great and David didn't seem that happy either.'

While Gulpilil showered after the rehearsal, Ruddy parked his van in the bush, put the boards together and propped the complete canvas against the van.

'He came back and I introduced him to my Spanish mate and, because David had done a commercial in Spain several years earlier, it was an ice-breaker, which was perfect. David told us his story of rushing to the airport when he was leaving for Spain but having to swim back home across the river first, because he'd forgotten his passport.'

Ruddy stood Gulpilil on a milk crate, made two quick charcoal sketches, and then started working straight onto the wallpapered boards.

'Within fifteen minutes, David saw himself. He said, "Brother, that's me! That's me!"' says Ruddy. 'I kept drawing and ten minutes later, I could feel someone behind me and there was a young girl taking photos and then the director and half the crew were there. They all ended up watching and they were excited to see David happy. They told me, "That's the first smile we've seen on his face for a month. You're not going anywhere. You're staying here for dinner." I kept working on the piece for another hour and then that was it. We hung out, went swimming down the river with David and the whole crew. The vibe had shifted and they ended up continuing with the show and going to Adelaide.'

Why does Ruddy believe it was his arrival that shifted the dynamic?

'David saw his likeness in the work immediately, so did everyone else. We were channelling the life force into it. I then had less than two weeks to get it back to the studio and finish it. I was working on it intensely, one day on, one day off, but the original structure never shifted.'

What was he trying to express in the work? The memory animates Ruddy. He lifts from his little bar stool, breathes in, inflates his chest, makes jazz hands.

'I wanted to express that power and dignity and strength and pride, and for me it was being a little bit of a rebel, bringing Indigenous culture to the dining table of Admiralty House, the governing body, to discuss issues and make a change. I saw it more as quite graffiti-style, like a kid rebelling and drawing on a wall. That was the fun side of it. But when we started chatting, when we had a break, smoked a joint and connected further on a deeper level, David was so excited. He was, like, "Yeah! We've got to travel all over the world with it. We'll travel all over Australia, and then the world, all the major landmarks. You do my portrait here, you do my portrait there," and then he was talking about wanting to do his face on the side of mountains. Later, a few journalists would speak about the solid-stone look, like he was part of a mountain.'

Ruddy and Agustin stayed for dinner and then till midnight, looking at books and photos and sharing stories before having to navigate their way out of the bush.

'The funniest thing, which is off the record ... [Ruddy pauses and thinks – for isn't expression everything to the artist?] ... *maybe not*, was my mate from Spain. He was the biggest stoner, this young, fun, blond curly-haired, blue-eyed Spanish wild man. After dinner David asked me to come to his room. He reached under his bed and pulled out a bucket bong. I could smoke a little bit but not that much and we'd already had a couple of joints. We were in the middle of the bush and I had to drive home. There was no way I could do that. So I said, "Hey Agustin!" He'd never done one before, never even heard of the concept. He had his first bucket bong with a legend. It was already an intense experience for him, but after that ...'

Ruddy and Agustin, their gourds up in smoke, eventually made it back to the three-bedroom high-rise apartment they shared at Tamarama, on Sydney's eastern beaches.

Now, Ruddy had to finish the work.

'The painting took up the entire living space overlooking the valley and the ocean. Creating the work there was intense. It was already powerful. I was covered in goosebumps most of the time and so was Agustin. To be honest, there was so much energy in the work it was overwhelming. Also a lot of pent up anger and frustration that I'd felt my whole life for the way Indigenous people had been treated here was being channelled into the work.'

He says it became so 'powerful and intense' that he couldn't sleep in the apartment.

'I'd drive my van down to the beach, to sleep and rest there and then go back to the apartment and work intensely on it further. Agustin was living with me at the time and sleeping on the day bed and rolling joint after joint. And the joints were getting bigger and bigger. It was a fun and exciting process but all too consuming. At that stage, my art dealers had been in to see the work and they were all, "Wow, it's incredible. Whatever you do, don't touch it." But we'd smoke a joint and I'd be laying there and be, like, "Nah, it's not him yet, it needs more." And this wave of energy would come over me and I'd jump up and frantically work on it for hours. To the point where Agustin flipped out. "You're crazy, man! You're crazy! You're not meant to touch it!" He had to escape from the apartment as well. It completely took on a life of its own.'

At five minutes to 4 pm on the Friday afternoon of the very last day submissions were accepted for the Archibald, Ruddy and his crew arrived at the National Gallery and poured out of his van.

'We had to carry it into the space and screw the whole thing together in the delivery area. These crazy kids working away. And I remember all the workers sitting there watching, quite complacent, you could see they were thinking, "C'mon, we want to go home", until we put the pieces together. They looked at each other, like, "*Whoa!*" That night it was on every TV channel.'

Two weeks later, *Two Worlds* was chosen as a finalist in a packed field that included portraits from the noted artists David Bromley, Adam Cullen and Ben Quilty.

Ruddy says that 'as a kid I knew of the Archibald but I'd been told stories that you need to be entering for at least five years before they even look at your work let alone be selected as a finalist. I knew it was a strong piece though and I was confident it would be selected as a finalist. But I knew I had no chance of winning. I was a complete unknown. But then, after it was selected as a finalist and it was at the forefront of all the media coverage, that's when I started panicking, thinking, "There *is* a chance of winning." Which was amazing but extremely confronting as I'd only been painting full time for two years. I was still establishing myself as an artist and I knew how controversial the Archibald can be and how brutal and critical most people can be of any work that wins.'

Ruddy was, as he impolitely puts it, 'shitting myself'.

'But I knew it was out of my hands. It had its own power and its own story and it was about to do its own thing. So, even to the day they were announcing the winner, I was unexpectedly late arriving to the Art Gallery of New South Wales. The whole media room was jam-packed so I had to be squeezed in at the back of the room with my friends while we waited for the announcement. When they said I'd won, a few people in the room said they saw my energy shoot through the roof... *whoosh!* ... and then it was like entering another world, an out-of-body experience, really. Security had to push their way through to me and clear a path so I could get to the lectern then the artwork. Everyone was ecstatic, microphones were in my face. I was, literally, pinned to the painting while the journalists were like seagulls. It was crazy.'

As daunting as it was, Ruddy was sharp in his description of the work.

'David is a man who crosses the lines that still divide two contrasting worlds. One is an infinite world of spiritual connection with the land and universe as a whole, and the other a materialistic conformation of Western civilisation. Simplicities and complexities infiltrate both worlds and David seems to strike a balance ... The bold, free-spirited line work of the charcoal and graphite contrast with the structured and refined opulence of the colonial English wallpaper.

I hope that the work represents the energy and spirituality that I experienced in his presence...'

The first prize was $35,000, a significant slice for a young artist on the make and with an inflated credit card debt. It also delivered an immediate and bankable fame.

'Things were already pretty good. I had a following and a client base, but the win took it to another level,' he says.

The following day, Ruddy called Gulpilil, who was home in Ramingining.

'At the time, I was a nobody, just a kid from the bush,' says Ruddy, who had originally hoped to visit Gulpilil in Ramingining to do his portrait. 'There were no expectations but things didn't evolve the way I'd hoped. David was so excited and happy and there was the potential of doing work together in the future but he seemed overwhelmed and a little incoherent at times. He'd been going through a bad stage around then. I had made previous plans to go live in Spain for a while and I decided to stick to my plans.'

Two Worlds wasn't finished.

After taking the main prize it also scooped the People's Choice award. Another artist, Tony Johansen, who'd entered a portrait of the transgender cabaret performer Carlotta but didn't make the final, commenced court proceedings on the basis that Ruddy's portrait was a drawing, not a painting, and therefore ineligible to win. The Sydney businessman Paul Haege kicked off Johansen's 'Archibald Challenge 2004 Fighting Fund' with a $1500 donation.

The painter Margaret Olley supported the case and said Ruddy's portrait was 'more a drawing than a painting'.

'The first news I got of it, he was trying to sue me directly.' says Ruddy.

Action was commenced in the New South Wales Supreme Court against both the Art Gallery of New South Wales Trust (as trustees for the relevant trust set up under Archibald's will) and against Ruddy.

'It was one month after winning the prize and the first I heard of it was when I was woken early in the morning by a phone call from the media room of the Art Gallery of New South Wales. She was, like, "Craig, I can't explain everything right now, but I suggest you don't answer the door to anyone, don't take any calls till you hear back from me." I was left in limbo for an hour or so, wondering what could be happening. She then called back, "We're being sued, the artwork is evidence for the courtroom. It's advised that you don't say a thing about the work to anyone until the hearing and you'll need to meet with lawyers this week." There was a brief discussion further about what was happening and that was it.'

The case spent two years winding through the legal labyrinth, ending up in the New South Wales Supreme Court, where Johansen's lawyer, Chris Burch, SC, said the rules of the Archibald stipulated that the prize must go to the 'best portrait painting, preferentially of some man or woman distinguished in art, letters, science or politics' by any artist in Australasia in the past twelve months.

'The legal question,' said Birch, 'is whether it can be described as having been painted.'

For Ruddy it meant two things. He couldn't sell the painting that was the talk of the town, and he was bound, legally, to keep his mouth shut.

'Before I even finished the work I had someone wanting to buy the piece. But I refused to sell it. They kept pressing to buy the work and the offer kept going up. Then, obviously, being a finalist, there were other people interested. And then once winning the prize, there were more people interested and a couple of government bodies. It was too overwhelming so I put a letter out to everyone stating that no decision would be made without giving everyone equal opportunity. The painting then became evidence in court so I couldn't do anything with it anyway,' he says. 'Journalists were always trying to get me to talk about it. At the pub, at a party or down the beach. I was going for a swim at Tamarama one day and a mate was coming out of the water. We stopped and were chatting and he was, like, "Do you know that person?" I turned around and there was someone standing there at the water's edge, fully clothed, with a pad in their hand ready for an interview . . .'

Ruddy says 'that first year was a bit disturbing. It was a head-fuck, you could say. The second year it became comical.'

As for the court case, 'The artwork is a mixed media work, it crossed all boundaries and could be classified as both a painting and a drawing. The prize goes to the best portrait,' says Ruddy. 'It was considered by many as the best portrait of the year, first and foremost. As court was adjourned so the judge could decide on a verdict, the funniest thing happened . . . after two days of the hearing, someone said to the judge, "Excuse me, your honour, about the evidence, can we remove it from the courtroom?" And the judge casually said, "You mean the painting?" The entire room gasped, and chuckled . . . "*Ohhhhhhhhhh!*"'

The judge eventually ruled that whether a piece of art was painted or not was simply a matter of opinion.

'Because of my conclusion that the portrait cannot be excluded from the category of a work which has been "painted", it cannot be said that the trustee's exercise of judgement or opinion was wrong,' he said in his judgment in 2006. 'There is a certain appearance of strangeness in courts making determinations concerning the qualities of works of art. The matter is better left to those in the art world.'

'It's a victory for art in general,' Ruddy said outside court. 'I don't think art should be judged in the courtroom and I think that was made very clear today.'

The two-year wait and the publicity the legal case generated drove the price of *Two Worlds* into the clouds.

Selling the work, says Ruddy, 'was too much for me to deal with, really, and I ended up speaking with Justin Miller from Sotheby's (who would compare *Two Worlds* to Sir William Dobell's 1943 *Portrait of an Artist*), and he agreed the best opportunity was to open it and put it to auction'.

Estimates ranged from $150,000 to $200,000. One month earlier, a landscape by Ruddy called *Remnants Scarlett* had sold for $20,000.

'I created it to make a statement,' Ruddy said when asked if he'd miss *Two Worlds*. 'I didn't create it to sit on my wall.'

Still, he didn't want *Two Worlds* to languish in the storeroom of a millionaire looking for a bulwark against inflation.

'It was a bit disturbing and risky but Justin assured me that he'd make sure it went to a good buyer. And it did. To a very respectful couple that were all about preserving prominent artwork for the future.'

Was Ruddy a little surprised at the bullish result?

'Yeah, completely surprised,' Ruddy says, wrapping it in an I-still-can't-believe-it laugh. 'Most Archibald works are very difficult to sell, they're quite unique pieces. It was a real shock to everyone.'

As part of the sale, Ruddy pledged to donate twenty per cent of the sale price to Indigenous causes, which turned out to be a not insignificant $52,000.

'I was very unwell as a child,' says Ruddy, 'and spent a lot of time with doctors and in hospitals. I wanted to contribute in some way to education opportunities and Indigenous medical students in the Northern Territory. Especially where David is from.'

How about Gulpilil? Did he see a little of the prize money?

'I gave David some of the money,' says Ruddy. 'At the time of winning the $35,000 prize I didn't have a cent to my name, but he wanted me to help him out to move a four-wheel drive across country and a few other things.'

I ask Ruddy what he saw when he first sketched Gulpilil, out there in the bush on the Hawkesbury River sixty clicks northwest of Sydney, in the land of the Darug nation.

'He was the most beautiful, beautiful man. Powerful, strong and full of charisma. Incredible cheekbones and with all that wild hair, he had the perfect look for the work and the image that came through. David's legacy is of the first-ever positive Indigenous role model in film. He's got the most expressive face and the theatrics that go with it. No one comes close to him. I remember at the time of painting him, we started chatting, and he seemed to morph into this beautiful symmetry with his motions and his movement.'

Ruddy waves both his arms and hands in circles.

'You can't explain or describe it. It was the most powerful, enigmatic thing. I remember this sense of knowing come over me, a feeling of calm belonging.'

One of the reasons Ruddy and Roberto are in Sydney is to photograph *Two Worlds*, to create an archival image, so it can be preserved as well as reproduced. When it was entered into the Archibald, the Art Gallery of New South Wales printed thousands of postcards and posters.

But that was well over a decade ago.

'I've been getting emails lately about the original posters fading and deteriorating,' says Ruddy. 'And the work is all around the world. An old flatmate called me up from France to tell me that she had just been to this little town right in the middle of the country to pick up something from a friend of her aunty's. The elderly woman had a framed postcard of *Two Worlds* by her bed. My flatmate screamed, "Where did you get that? My friend painted that!" The woman told her a friend of a friend had sent the postcard and that she kept it by the bed because she loves it so much and that it empowers her. The image is scattered around the world.'

As the original sits in all its splendour in the foyer of the art collector couple's house in Sydney's Bellevue Hill, back in Murray Bridge, the old poster is wrapped in frameless glass and propped up on a table at the entry to the home of David Gulpilil and Mary Hood. A present to Mary from Gulpilil, a twenty-five-centimetre 'cheeky farting gnome' who is bent over, with pants down, two double-A batteries providing the electricity for his motion-activated farts, acts as a sentinel.

Gulpilil gazes at the portrait with soft eyes.

'That's me!' he says. 'We won the prize!'

— CHAPTER 7 —

A Famous Artist Paints a Portrait of the Old Man

I HAVEN'T BEEN SO BARKED AT IN YEARS. THE ARTIST and documentary filmmaker George Gittoes, famous for painting Julian Assange in his Ecuadorean embassy hidey-hole, having a pistol fired point-blank at his head while taunting the Taliban with provocative song and dance in Pakistan (the Chinese-made Beretta jammed), escaping execution at the hands of Rwandan Patriotic Army president Paul Kagame and his soldiers in the Congo, and who tells a harrowing story of fighting a Great White shark off the coast of Galveston, Texas, really lets me have it.

Gittoes is sixty-eight years old. He wears head-to-toe black (of course – artist!), and his head is crowned by a waterfall of silver hair that browns at the ends. A beard, also silver, is trimmed to a point, and what skin remains visible amid the grove of hair is as pink as an oriental sunset.

'This... *place*... has a puritanical emptiness like Stavanger in Norway,' he says, vibrating a masculine intensity despite being the size of an adolescent girl. 'David Gulpilil is a highly cultured, highly sophisticated person who's played a part in the history of Australian film and dance and drama and everything else. I rang some people connected with David in his own country, they all knew I was coming here, and they said, if he's got terminal cancer, he's gotta get home. There's things you have to do when an old tribal man like him is near the end. There's rituals that have got to be performed and for the ongoing passing of their souls and joining the spirit world. But when I said that David may be gone in the next few months they said it would be terrible if he ended up ending his days in . . .'

Gittoes raised four Aboriginal kids and took 'em through their tribal initiation. He pauses and peers around, searching for a street sign to identify the town.

'What's this place called?'

Murray Bridge.

'Yeah. [Flatly] *Murray Bridge*. And in an environment where . . . now I don't want someone to read your writing and have me putting down Mary, probably the only person in the world that cares for him and who's looking after him, but that's separate to what a tragedy it would be for him to end his life as far from his own culture as he could get.'

Gittoes stares at me.

The bark turns into a bite.

'YOU! have to drive him home.'

Gittoes and I have flown to Adelaide and driven to Murray Bridge so he can draw and paint a portrait of Gulpilil, someone he says he has a forty-year connection to.

'David will remember me,' he says.

FADE IN: It's 1976 and Gittoes, twenty-six, is shooting lifestyle footage in Arnhem Land for the upcoming Philippe Mora movie *Mad Dog Morgan*. The camera zooms in on Gittoes at Maningrida homestead watching an Aboriginal dance troupe.

'David did the most inspired dance I've ever seen in my life. It was up there with Nureyev and Graeme Murphy. David does dances, particularly where he uses his hands and eyes, and brings his legs together, where he actually evokes another dimension. It's spirit stuff, way, way above the heads of the tourists who were watching who would've liked the animal mimicry stuff, the emu, the kangaroo.'

Gittoes says the South African man who ran the troupe and announced each act ('Some sort of African boer') was so outrageously patronising it made his blood pressure soar.

'It was genuinely insulting,' he says. 'I had a similar experience getting on the plane yesterday in Sydney. A whole group of Aboriginal women had been to something and they were in the queue but other people just kept on pushing in front of 'em. I was behind them and they were letting all these people through and I said, 'Come on, ladies! Don't let them push in!' And so the ladies asserted themselves. But they were reticent about asserting themselves, and when we were walking down the air bridge they turned around and laughed at me and winked. They were really glad but they needed that bit of encouragement. They're such a downtrodden race they weren't going to say anything. They were going to let everybody on the plane before them and people were prepared to do it.'

At Maningrida, 'all the tourists and everyone else were prepared to let this arsehole insult David. I went up and confronted him and it went beyond words. We went toe to toe and we threw a few punches, which David saw, but this guy had his people and I was on my own, and they broke it up. It was good that they did. I'm a trained fighter and I could've got myself into a lot of trouble. But David was delighted. A day or two later, somewhere between Katherine and Maningrida, tribe country, where you have to have a permit to enter, I saw a lean-to with a bit of tarp thrown over it. That's where David was sleeping, this superstar from *Walkabout*. Here he is in his own country and he's just a dancing boy sleeping out in the open. Around the same time, Polaroid presented [Australian photographer]

Jonny Lewis and I and a few others, including Andy Warhol in America, gold plated SX-70 cameras as a gesture of appreciation. You're supposed to treasure it for life and here's David, who's been given one, and it's sitting out in the rain along with a whole lot of other valuable things like a cassette tape recorder, which were as rare as hen's teeth in those days. And they were all ruined by the rain. He didn't give a shit.'

I meet Gittoes at Adelaide airport. He'd planned on covering the cost of the trip by reinvigorating an unused ticket to Adelaide. On the way to Sydney's domestic airport from his beachfront house in Werri Beach, a couple of hours south, he blew a tyre and missed the flight.

Bought another ticket, this time at full freight. The trip costs him a thousand dollars.

'Call David and let him know we'll be late,' Gittoes says. 'Tell him there's been some *humbug*. That's how Aboriginals describe it. He'll understand.'

It's lucky Gulpilil is here at all.

Three weeks earlier, Mary had found him slumped in his plastic shower chair. Gulpilil has lost his famous hunter's power, so Mary has to operate the tap and before she turns it off she asks him if it's okay 'cause she knows how he likes to let the water run off his face. When she asked three times and he didn't respond, Mary pulled back the shower curtain.

Gulpilil was still. No breath. No pulse.

Mary yelled for her son Tony to call the ambulance and ran to the bedroom to get the oxygen concentrator, a box on wheels that converts air to oxygen by removing the nitrogen.

Mary, the nurse, stuffed the two plastic prongs into his nostrils.

Hit the start button. The oxygen flowed.

The Old Man stirred.

In Adelaide, George navigates us to an art supply store. He buys four cans of spray paint, red, white, a regular sorta blue and a cobalt blue, plus jars of red and black acrylic. He buys crayons and a one-and-a-half-metre high canvas that is stretched over a wooden frame.

The cobalt blue is a nod to his old friend Martin Sharp, with whom he co-founded the creative commune the Yellow House in Sydney's King Cross, and who painted Gulpilil blue in 2012.

Sharp's portrait of Gulpilil was called, at Gulpilil's insistence, *The Thousand Dollar Bill*.

'He requested that the portrait be my design for the thousand dollar bill,' Sharp said at its unveiling. 'David felt keenly the disparity of what he was paid as an actor and the other actors who were paid so much more.'

A nod to Sharp, but it had to be blue anyway, says Gittoes.

'I've always seen David's aura as blue. It just is. I've always had the disability of seeing these things. Martin was a mystic too, I think.'

Later, he'll point to the blue as fitting with the colour of Gulpilil's eyes.

'Extraordinary for a full-blooded Aboriginal,' says Gittoes.

When I tell him that the blue rings on the outside of his pupils are cataracts he says, 'They may be cataracts but I prefer to believe they are his real colour.

'I have known other Aboriginals from his region with blue eyes. Aboriginals are Caucasian.'

The stretched canvas occupies two-thirds of the car, fitting inside with only a couple of millimetres gap on each side of the frame. Gittoes is alive with stories on the hour-and-a-half to Murray Bridge.

He tells of losing laptops to the CIA, who are eternally suspicious of his dealings with the Taliban and with that gadfly Julian Assange, why Gittoes uses a succession of 'burner' phones (the CIA steals smartphones off the people it's spying on, says Gittoes), and the elevation of life when you're forever close to death.

We park kerbside out the front of the driveway that leads to Gulpilil and Mary's townhouse.

'How do you want to do this?' asks Gittoes.

We briefly discuss the best way to arrive with canvases, cameras and so on, lest we appear wolfish, white men gobbling our piece of this Australian icon.

Still, Gittoes can't resist the theatre of a grand entrance. He drapes himself in a satin jacket with electric blue taping down each arm that he bought in Englewood on Chicago's Southside where he's filming a documentary called *White Light* about desperate young gangsters.

Reaching into his suitcase he fills his paws with cameras, a bag of pencils, crayons and paints and steps out of the car as if he is walking out on stage.

Two doors slam.

The old Yolngu man is camped, as is his habit, in front of the gas heater in the townhouse's front room. The blind is three-quarters shut to keep the east-facing morning sun at bay. The TV plays Netflix's neo-Blaxploitation series *Luke Cage*, about an African-American superhero in Harlem.

Gittoes will attach significance to the black Australian watching the black American superhero ('Did you *see* what he was watching?' he'll whisper), but it'll turn out that it's a favourite of Mary's white, middle-aged son Tony, who shares the townhouse.

Gulpilil has spent the last two weeks being treated for pneumonia in the Royal Adelaide Hospital. Mary likes the rooms there, says it's like being in a hotel, and the window, which overlooks Adelaide Oval, has box seating 'with cushions as big as a lounge' that can be made up into a bed.

After the shower episode, doctors had run tests and found he was suffering from a double hit of pneumonia, viral and bacterial.

'As soon as he got there, they put an IV drip of antibiotics straight in,' says Mary.

Two days home and Gulpilil's not in great shape. It might be mid-spring but the temperature isn't budging above thirteen. He wears a polar fleece jacket over T-shirt and shirt and black jeans and boots. An R.M. Williams belt secures the jeans to Gulpilil's distinct outline.

'David's a tropical fish, he's not a cold water fish,' Gittoes tells Mary, who nods politely.

We all take our places in the front room, Gulpilil and Mary in the prized side-by-side armchairs facing the heater and television, me on a footstool and Gittoes on a three-seater couch decorated with a red rose motif.

There's silence.

Gulpilil is barely here. His bottom lip, distended from the cancer treatment, hangs loose. His eyes close at regular intervals, a side-effect of the opioid Endone he's taking as part of his pain management for cancer.

'Sick, very sick, yeah, just come out of hospital,' he apologises.

Gittoes tries to revive him with the old story of belting the South African in Maningrida.

'You know, you and I met back in 1976,' says Gittoes.

'Yeah,' gasps Gulpilil, breath shortened by double pneumonia and the tumours in his lungs.

'You were a dancer at Maningrida homestead...'

'Yeah, yeah...'

Gittoes pokes around, trying to push a button that might turn on the lights. Talks about the SX-70 rusting out in the open at Gulpilil's lean-to ('Yeah, on the road there,' says Gulpilil), about going home ('It's been a while') and a mutual friend, the didgeridoo virtuoso David Blanasi, from whom Gittoes bought a didge. ('He's dead. Been gone a long time.')

Eventually, Gittoes turns to Mary.

'So, you're looking after this treasure, this wonderful man...'

'Yes.'

'How's he going?'

Mary pats Gulpilil on the arm.

'How are you travelling, all right aren't you David?'

'Still the best looking man in Australia,' charges Gittoes.

Silence.

Gittoes won't be thwarted.

'Still having to bat all the girls off?'

Another pat on Gulpilil's arm.

'We mainly keep to ourselves a bit, don't we? Yeah.'

If this were a comedy club, it'd be raining tomatoes.

Gittoes gets to the point.

'I'm going to try and do a beautiful portrait of David. Do you remember dear old Martin Sharp? Martin and I were the closest friends. Martin did the best portrait of David ever.'

Mary replies that they've still got a small print of the portrait, which was subsequently wrapped in plastic and stored away somewhere after it started to get holes in it.

'The year that Martin put that in the Archibald it was the best painting there by a million miles and they gave it to some boring picture,' says Gittoes. 'And it broke Martin's heart. I went up to the judges and said, "Why didn't you give the prize to Martin?" and they said, yeah, they should've but, for some reason, they had a mental block and realised their mistake later.'

Gittoes looks back at Gulpilil.

'What's your totem, David? King brown? Kangaroo?'

Every Aboriginal clan has a totem, an object, an animal, fish or plant, that is their spiritual emblem.

Gulpilil's are a python and water goanna.

'Who was your *jungai*?'

'Who is my *what*?'

'The bloke who taught you everything.'

'I can't remember.'

'Did you ever meet your grandparents?'

'I didn't see my grandfather but he left a message for me at a ceremony.'

Gulpilil starts to doze.

Suddenly, he wakes with a start.

'*Mary! Mary!*'

Mary is unflappable.

'I'm here! What's the matter?'

'*Get my painting!*'

———

The action, if you wanna call it that given its mass shuffle and glacial pace, shifts to the kitchen and dining area of the house. Mary appears with a three-metre-long plastic tube containing two of Gulpilil's paintings, which he wants to show Gittoes.

Gulpilil opens the tube and pulls out the two canvases, which Gittoes and I help unfurl. Both measure two metres by one metre. The first is a pool of various browns, with water lilies and various fish.

Gulpilil's voice deepens. He stands tall. He's into this.

'Ah yeah. It's a story. Barramundi and catfish,' he says, in a salesman-like manner. 'The other is bream fish. Unfinished.'

Later, Gittoes will explain the painting's significance.

'David is catfish dreaming and totem. The four catfish are meant to represent different stages of his life as they shelter under lily pads protected by small green water pythons and four little turtles. A single white and yellow lily flower blossoms at the top like a little sun.'

Gittoes takes photos of Gulpilil with his paintings. Gulpilil automatically turns his head to profile when the camera comes out. ('Notice how all the good photos are taken in profile,' Gittoes explains.) Eyes flare open.

We all stand and stare at the paintings laid out on the tiled floor.

Later, Gittoes will explain to me that this wasn't a courtesy call, a proud artist showing off his work.

He wants to sell 'em.

Three years earlier, ABC Darwin had found Gulpilil selling his work outside a shopping mall.

"'I had to come back to Darwin to do painting of my country and I'm really happy here in Darwin," Gulpilil said ...

'Press and red carpet premieres will come, but right now Gulpilil is happy painting on canvas. He hopes to one day make good money from his works.

"'$50,000 that's all right, it's only small,' he said with a cheeky grin.

"'Come here anyway and see me painting.

"'Right here in the middle of Darwin — Darwin mall mate.'"

'Now,' announces Mary. 'Is it all right if George does a little sketch of you? Want to sit in the lounge?'

Back in the front room, George whips out his paper and his crayons with a flourish and starts sketching and taking more photos. Gulpilil, warmed by the heater and the welcoming softness of his elephantine lounge chair, drifts in and out of sleep.

In his moments of lucidity, I interview, asking questions about growing up in Arnhem Land in the time before his life was changed by the moving picture.

I get a few scattered riffs on *Walkabout* and its British director Nicolas Roeg.

'I was a dancer, dancing boy... Nicolas Roeg... he saw me. I like dancing in films.'

On his mission name, David.

'I hated it. It took me a long time to get used to it.'

Gittoes works away with his camera and sketches. He moves a dozing Gulpilil's hands here and there for dramatic effect. Gulpilil will spring into life for thirty seconds, tilt his head, stare into the camera and own it, then fall back asleep.

Soon, Gittoes has what he needs. He plans on taking the sketches and photos back to our motel room and transferring it to the giant canvas. He wants Gulpilil to see an almost finished portrait in the morning.

'Before I leave,' Gittoes tells Gulpilil, 'I'm going to give you some of my white magic.'

White magic? Who has ever heard of such a thing?

Gittoes embraces Gulpilil in a manner that is, despite its strangeness and awkwardness, neither strange nor awkward.

'White magic,' says Gittoes, eyes locked onto Gulpilil's pools of black, ringed by the pale blue cataracts.

Gittoes moves his face back so Gulpilil can see the full import of his words.

'And maybe you need to go home...'

The Adelaide Road Motor Lodge is an accidental slice of modernist Palm Springs in a town that is one long colonial riff. A stone facade out front. Floor-to-ceiling glass. Notes of cubism.

Participants at a classic car rally have booked out most of the motel, each room with a restored Ford Model A parked outside.

Gittoes gets the deluxe family unit down a side road, which is neither modernist nor Palm Springs, more regional Australia meets low-cost housing bathed in muted tones of beige, and spreads out his paints and canvas and sketches inside the kitchen and television room.

He works throughout the afternoon and into the night.

When I come to get him for dinner, the canvas is propped up on a side table, an empty jar of black acrylic and paintbrushes nearby. There's still the colour to fill in, a plastic bag full of spray cans is testimony to its final vision, but the black-and-white painting is an arresting moment of the Old Man at the end of his life.

Gulpilil stares at the viewer, the familiar bulldog nose ('Like an F-series Holden,' says Gittoes), long hair and beard, in a flash of, what?

Defiance?

Accusation?

Love?

'I love Australia. I love its flavour,' Gulpilil poetically claimed years ago.

While living in New York in the late sixties and early seventies, Gittoes fell under the spell of the great African-American figurative artist Joe Delaney.

'I'm the perfect artist to paint David because I've done a lot of other portraits of Aborigines. But my closest friend in America was Joe. And Joe taught me to draw the human figure and the human face,' says Gittoes. 'I'm working with a totally different physiognomy, different facial structures. It's not easy for white people to draw and paint black people. But I've now had fifty years of doing it. With David, usually you can't see his eyes, only a glint, white laser beams coming out of those very dark, deep eye sockets.'

Gittoes admits to terrible nerves while drawing Gulpilil.

'I didn't know if I had stage fright, I was like a nervous nellie. I didn't want to disappoint David but he's got such a strong spirit it turned out to be an easy thing to do.'

Gittoes gets up at five-thirty the following morning and takes the canvas outside to apply the spray paints. He doesn't normally use spray paint, he prefers to use only acrylics, but he wanted to be able to take the painting off its frame, roll it up and take it back to his Werri Beach studio to work on it some more.

And, he says, the spray cans act in ways not unlike techniques employed by traditional Arnhem Land artists.

'They actually put white ochre in their mouths and spit it out. They become a human spray can,' says Gittoes. 'So it's appropriate to do David with spray paint and brush work.'

Inside the unit, plastic sheets are strewn across tables and in the kitchen. Crayons and paints litter the floor.

'I paint on the hop and quite often do my best work in hotels and motels,' says Gittoes. 'I've trashed more hotel rooms than Oasis.'

By 9 am, the work, with Gulpilil's face blue coming out of a fire engine red background, is finished enough to take around to show its subject. On the way to the nurse and the movie star's townhouse, we stop off at a bank so Gittoes can withdraw $2000 in cash.

He wants to buy Gulpilil's barramundi and catfish painting.

'How much should I offer?' asks Gittoes.

I tell him if he's prepared to sling the whole two gees, then start at $1500. Gulpilil knows his way around a negotiation.

Back at the townhouse, Gittoes marches the frame into the house. The sun is a little warmer today. So is the welcome.

'You're looking a lot better today, healthy. You got a little bit of my white magic yesterday,' says Gittoes.

Gulpilil is animated.

'Yeah! Yeah! *Gimme more!*'

'I'll give you more. I can do that. I got that magic,' says Gittoes. 'That's probably the real reason why I came down here.'

All five of us, Mary, Gulpilil, Tony, Gittoes and I, move outside to examine the canvas in the daylight. I take photos of George and David with the canvas. Mary and David. Tony and George. Mary and George and so on, until every combination is exhausted.

'I've got something interesting to tell you, David,' announces Gittoes. 'This boy here, it's his birthday today!'

Gulpilil looks at me in side profile.

Broad smile.

Then, loudly, 'What about we give him one present! For his birthday, we give him one!'

Gittoes has brought the two sketches he made yesterday, one in blue, one in black.

He offers Gulpilil his choice of sketch. He chooses the black-and-white. The pair present me with the blue sketch.

'I've signed it. You should sign it too,' Gittoes tells Gulpilil.

A black ink pen is fetched and passed to the Old Man at the dining table. His signature is practised, a flourish of D and G, suffixed with OAM, the Medal of the Order of Australia he won in 1987 for 'service to the arts through the interpretation of Aboriginal culture'.

'I want to give him the other one, too, the photograph,' hoots Gulpilil, getting into the birthday giving spirit.

I'm despatched to his bedroom to find and bring out another cylinder. I ask Mary if it's okay if I have a look around and examine the movie star's bedroom. Mary's a rare soul for whom transparency is as natural as the setting of the sun and she waves me in the direction of the room muttering, 'Of course, of course.'

If the reader will leave any privacy concerns outside this

volume and permit a voyeuristic detour, I'll guide you through the fore cabin.

First, we mark out its size. It is five by three metres with an ensuite bathroom off its western limb. A queen-sized bed has matching bedspread and pillow cases, each decorated with nineteenth-century illustrations of flower seed packets: rose, wild meadow mix, primula sinensis and so on.

The top of a black wooden table near the door, and flanking a television facing the bed, is populated with jars of coconut body butter, beard oil, shea butter cream, mint and tea tree shower gel, a Vaseline body moisturiser, a choc mint soy travel candle and a gold hurricane lamp with the globe missing.

A table under the window has two scented candles, a black, broad-brimmed leather hat with feathers, Gulpilil's centenary medal, which is kept in a box (there are actually two medals inside, one large, one small, and a commemorative fifty-cent piece), a plastic beaker for measuring medicine and his 2014 award for best actor at the Un Certain Regard section of the Cannes festival for *Charlie's Country*, a star with a diamond at the centre. Cannes has proved fruitful for the Rolf de Heer/David Gulpilil combo. In 2006, the pair's film *Ten Canoes* won the special jury prize.

A chair is decorated with a pillow with stitched images of three pelicans under a yellow sun.

Near the bed is a Clement Clarke Medix AC2000 nebuliser, a machine that sends Ventolin straight into Gulpilil's lungs via a mist inhaled through an oxygen mask.

On the floor is the lifesaving oxygen concentrator.

The drawer of a bedside table is left open, revealing two torches, a wallet with a yellow-paint fingerprint and rusted metal sunglasses. Another bedside table has two of Gulpilil's black broad-brimmed leather hats mounted on a fringed table lamp.

Below, three pairs of orthopaedic slippers.

I find the large plastic tube and bring it into the dining room for the unveiling of the treasure contained within.

The tube is opened and two large posters of the movie *Charlie's Country*, with the credits written in French, are spread across the tiles. The poster's photo shows Gulpilil with three spears and his woomera and wearing a sleeveless flannel shirt. His right bicep bulges with a topography like the Arnhem Land hills. Gulpilil's physical beauty, even at sixty when the photo was taken, is difficult to overstate. His limbs are like weapons, coiled and ready to hunt, to dance, to act. A tendril of looped silver hair falls into his face. Either a late morning or afternoon sun wraps his head in a gold halo.

'This is for you,' says Gulpilil.

It's a fine birthday gift.

Gittoes steps into the frame.

'You know that painting that you had yesterday, your one, would you be interested in selling that one?'

'Yes, yes,' says Gulpilil, unsurprised.

'It's not *finished*,' says Mary.

'I know he needs a few bob,' says Gittoes.

'He does,' concedes Mary.

'I'm going to buy that one you showed me yesterday, the water lilies if I can. I've got a thousand bucks on me. Is that enough?'

There's confusion about what painting Gittoes wants. Gulpilil shows a portrait of him painted by a friend; another painting by his daughter.

'No, no, the one in the cylinder yesterday,' says Gittoes.

Gulpilil shows another painting.

'Don't want this one,' says Gittoes.

Mary is exasperated.

'No, not this one. *Your painting*,' she says. 'The one with the water lilies. *Pull 'em out again!*'

Again, I'm despatched to the bedroom. The paintings are retrieved from the plastic cylinder and unfurled.

'Now, what I'd like to do,' says Gittoes, pulling out his wallet and counting out twenty fifty-dollar bills. 'Is one thousand dollars enough? Or do you want some more?'

Gittoes wants to up the price to his two-gee limit. He has no interest in winning the negotiation.

'That's enough,' says Gulpilil, counting the notes.

'I'm another artist. I'm poor. Are you sure that's enough?'

Gulpilil thinks.

'One thousand seven hundred.'

'Give you another seven hundred?' smiles Gittoes.

'Yeah.'

Gittoes hands over fourteen more fifties.

Mary laughs.

'It's worth it! I've got no idea what he wants,' says Gittoes. 'The reason I want to do it is I want to put your painting next to mine when I put it in the museum. It won't stay with me. It'll go to a museum. It's very important.'

'He says his hand is too wobbly to paint any more. From chemo and stuff,' says Mary.

Gittoes changes tack.

'David. What has to happen is, we gotta get you back to Maningrida.'

'Mmmmm.'

'Back up north for a visit.'

Mary comes in. 'Yeah, but we have to wait till he finishes all this treatment.'

'I'd like to take you there,' says Gittoes. 'I know all those people. We'll do it and we'll have fun.'

'All right, yeah,' says Gulpilil, unconvincingly.

'When does the treatment finish, Mary?'

'The trial's for two years.'

'Yeah, but he can go before that can't he?'

'The doctor says that even if it [the immunotherapy trial] doesn't help David or only helps David a bit, because their DNA and everything is different to ours, it can help people in the future.'

'The thing is,' says George, 'If he had a visit back home it could do him as much good as the medicine. He needs it. I know he needs it. He needs to have a moment back home.'

Mary, gruffly, 'Yeah.'

'He's already looking better today.'

'His lungs are only working at forty per cent with the emphysema,' says Mary.

'So you think he could do a trip then?' asks Gittoes.

'We've discussed it many times, haven't we David?'

Gulpilil looks down at his hands.

'Yeah.'

'The thing was, too, last year he went to get on a bus and he couldn't do it because he was too closed in,' says Mary. 'Rolf [de Heer] and I discussed many ways to try and do it.'

'David, what if I got my car and we drove up and we took it bit by bit? You could come as well Mary, just drive up?'

'Wouldn't get too far down the road before he'd want to come back,' says Mary. 'His main fear is different doctors if he got sick and it's taken a *long* time for him to have confidence in the doctors. That's the main thing. He has to feel confident if I have to call another doctor. Not that I don't want to do it.'

Gittoes sees an opening.

'I think it would be very good for him to go.'

Mary throws her hands up in the air.

'So do I! So work it out!'

On the drive back to Adelaide airport, with short shrift given to sightseeing in historic Murray Bridge, Gittoes lays it out.

'I expected to see David not looking well because he'd just gotten out of hospital but today's meeting was terrific,' says Gittoes, buoyed. 'Yesterday he was drifting off on Endone and his bottom lip was popping out. I've had a lot of friends who've passed away with dementia around the same age, like Richard Neville, a man with the sharpest wit and the sharpest mind of my generation, so I was really worried that David was suffering from dementia. But I think he was just suffering from Endone and fragility in his lungs. Today he was very lucid and dear and I brought back some of his memories and I gave him a big hug and told him I want you to get better and be more positive. And today he reckoned it had worked. He wanted more and I gave him some more, whether you believe in that sort of thing or not. Yesterday I found it was awkward because I was trying to work out whether he was really on the edge of going into oblivion and today he's woken up a different man. So I'm going away happy.'

But, says Gittoes, 'I look at him here, people think, oh David Gulpilil is rolling in money, and he's paying 230 dollars a week to live in a dead-beat town because the rent's cheap. How many other movie stars of his stature in the world are living on nothing?'

Gittoes proposes approaching a philanthropist to cover the cost of getting Gulpilil back to Arnhem Land.

'We need to, and a lot of other people need to, help him so he can live better than he's living. I'm happy to donate a painting to do it. We should get the money and take him home in style and you should let people know the conditions he's living under. Recently, there was a hullabaloo about Albert Namatjira and how badly he was treated and now his work is selling for a fortune. In 2018, David Gulpilil shouldn't be in a $230 a week rented place in the back of buggery where there's no one from his own culture. That's wrong. We don't want a story coming out after he's died saying how terrible it was.'

Gittoes stops. Draws breath.

'He's alive *now*.'

― CHAPTER 8 ―

Paul Hogan Goes to an Alice Springs Casino, Meets Gulpilil

A HYSTERICAL DOG IS BELTING HIS LARGE SQUARE head through the screen-door bars of a brown-brick house of nineteen-seventies origin in an outer Sydney suburb called Belrose. He's nosed a hole in the fly-wire and is consumed by a desire to either lavish with tongue or consume the strange arrival at his door.

The dog's motivation, to either end, is unclear.

'C'mon, get in there! Jesus Christ!' barks the familiar long-faced actor and comic as he squeezes past the animal. 'He's not very bright... *g'arn get in there stupid!*'

Paul Hogan is back in Australia from Venice Beach in California where he lives with his son, Chance, to shoot the fourth instalment in the Crocodile Dundee series, *The Very Excellent Mr Dundee*.

'I don't like the title,' says the almost octogenarian, who was born on the same day Hitler annexed West Poland in 1939.

'I think it came from the Japanese,' grins the comic.

Hogan is lean and upright despite his age, the good condition of his physique obvious in fitted denim shirt and jeans. It shouldn't be a surprise. His mum Florence was born just after the turn of the twentieth century and died one hundred and one years later in 2010.

Are you funny in the new film?

'It's a comedy from start to finish, and it should be called *No Good Deed Goes Unpunished* because I end up in the shit,' says Hogan. 'Everything I do ends up wrong and I end being despised. It's ninety-five per cent finished. It's sorta like whatever happened to Crocodile Dundee? I'm playing myself. So's everyone. So's Mel [Gibson]. John Cleese is in it. Chevy Chase, all sorts of people coming in and out. Got Olivia Newton John, she's fabulous. Margot Robbie's got a little cameo in it. Eric Bana. All of 'em are my mates. They're doing it for peanuts and they all want to be in a funny movie and it's bloody funny. It's how people are trying to get me to make another *Dundee* and what happens and what bad ideas they have and how I end up being a national disgrace.

'Sit over 'ere,' says Hogan, indicating a wooden bench with cushions. A rectangular table is dominated by two packets of cigarettes, a lighter and an ashtray, which is full. The bench overlooks a bucolic front yard, its foliage decorated with surfboards, skateboards, exercise and gardening equipment. A wetsuit is hung over the front gate to dry.

This is the house of Hogan's daughter, Lauren, one of his five kids to Noelene, whom he married in 1958, divorced in 1981, remarried in 1982 and divorced again in 1990.

Lauren has four boys in their twenties; Hogan is travelling with his sixth kid, Chance, who is nineteen, his son to *Crocodile Dundee* co-star Linda Kozlowski, whom he married in 1990 and divorced in 2014.

'It's like staying at the YMCA. The house isn't big enough for everyone, someone always has a mate or a girlfriend over, but I like to sleep on the floor,' he says. 'I've got an air mattress. I'd rather be here than in a hotel.'

It's very *Crocodile Dundee*, the surprise hit of 1986 that was the second-highest grossing film worldwide that year, only a couple of mill behind *Top Gun*, and stomping *Platoon*, *Aliens* and *Ferris Bueller's Day Off*.

It's still the highest-grossing Australian film ever.

It's *Dundee* that put Hogan, then forty-seven, and Gulpilil, thirty-three, both at the top of their game, adored and instantly recognisable, side by side in one of the movie's great comedic moments.

SCENE: Mick Dundee and New York reporter Sue Charlton are in repose by a camp fire. Dundee hands Charlton a wet towel to clean a small wound on her upper ham.

'Want me to have a look at that?' says Dundee.

'It's just a scratch,' says Charlton.

'Yeah, well, a scratch can get septic out here. Give us a look,' says Dundee, pushing Charlton onto all fours and lifting her skirt to examine the wound, a Benny Hill-esque exchange that would give millennials an attack of the vapours, trembling fingers punching hysterical tweets, if it were screened today.

Noise.

Dundee disappears.

Charlton sees an Aboriginal man in face paint appear from behind a tree.

Ominous music plays. Gets louder.

Charlton panics.

'*Mick?*'

Dundee appears with a knife at the man's throat. Both smile.

Gulpilil is the Aboriginal man. He plays Neville Bell.

Neville: 'I'm on my way to corroboree. It's a bloody drag. But still, my dad get angry if I don't show up.'

Charlton pulls out her camera. Nev tells her she can't take his photograph.

'I'm sorry – you believe it will take your spirit away?'

Neville: 'No, you've got lens cap on.'

A few beats.

Charlton: 'How does he find his way in the dark?'

Dundee: 'He thinks his way. A lot of people believe that they're telepathic.'

We hear Nev trip in the dark.

Neville: 'Ooh! God, I hate the bush.'

'This is a fascinating scene for its cultural complexities,' wrote film critic Paul Byrnes. 'It makes fun of traditional white misunderstandings and cultural taboos ('You think it will steal your spirit?') but makes clear that such taboos exist and must be respected (when Sue raises, then lowers, her camera). There is also the idea that cities corrupt black men like Neville, who has lost touch with some of his culture.'

It almost never happened. Hogan was in Alice Springs shooting a Tourism Australia commercial in 1984 when he stopped for a drink and to chance his arm at Lasseters Casino.

The pair didn't know each other, personally, but everyone knew Hoges; everyone knew Gulpilil.

'I'd seen him in *Walkabout*,' says Hogan, 'but I wasn't in the film industry or television. I was just a punter looking at it. And I'd seen him dance on television. David was in the casino, and, well, shit, he says, "Paul, how are ya, mate?"'

'He was having a drink and looking around and as soon as I saw his head, I thought, you've gotta be in this movie.'

When he asked, Gulpilil turned on that million-buck smile and said, 'Oh yeah, I'll be in it.'

'So I wrote him into the film and he was just fabulous,' says Hogan. 'David's one of those guys you just look at, he grins, and you're friends. We'd never met but we hit it off straight away. He had a vitality about him. There's an instant, "I like this bloke". We did the movie and he gave it that unique Australian flavour because he represented so much of what this country originally was, what it was based on. Of the earth.'

Hogan grew up in Granville, a working-class suburb in western Sydney that was multicultural before the word existed, and says while he may not have had an encyclopedic knowledge of Aboriginal culture he was certainly 'aware of it'.

'The best man at my wedding was Aboriginal. My mate I grew up with, Black Les. That's what we called him because we had two Les's in our gang. He was Black Les and the other one was Silly Big Les. You'd ask, "Which Les?" Oh Black Les! Or, Silly Big Les! Our gang were from all over the place: a Thursday Islander, a half-Aboriginal, a Greek, an Italian, two Assyrians.'

A year later, after the teenage Hogan's marriage to Noelene in 1958, Black Les got married and Hogan was his best man.

'Neither of the marriages worked out in the long run,' says Hogan leaving behind the faintest trail of wistfulness.

At least he had a couple of swings with Noelene and, later, almost a quarter century with *Dundee* co-star Kozlowski.

'They [the marriages] were both good, for a while. They wear out. Nothing wrong with that.'

Hogan says Gulpilil did more than act on *Crocodile Dundee*. When he wanted a corroboree scene in the film, 'David said he'd fix it and he did. All the guys turned up. I loved working with David. He's a fun bloke. We loved having him in the camp. When he dances, wow, he goes into the whole spirit of the thing. It's like a thousand years old. And when you're in the Northern Territory, when you're in Arnhem Land, your mind goes back. There's a feel up there that's timeless, you know? And David was representing his people. People who owned this country. Our wonderful ancestors came in, shot 'em, drove 'em out and took possession as the English used to in those days. The arrogance of it. Chase 'em. Shoot 'em. A terrible arrogance and why the prime minister (John Howard) wouldn't apologise . . .'

Hogan trails off muttering, 'Well, it's in the past, I think it might mean we have to give 'em money, duh, duh, duh . . .'

Suddenly, and with passion, 'This was their country, this . . . *is* . . . their country, right, their civilisation never changed over forty thousand years. They never invented the wheel and they never built villages and that sorta thing but they discovered aerodynamics!'

The boomerang! The first man-made object heavier than air able to fly!

'It's based on the physical principal of aerodynamics and no other country did that. And think of the woomera, extending your arm! There's a physics in that!'

Hogan becomes exasperated.

'They never invented the wheel but they were ... they *exploited* ... aerodynamics! They're of the earth. They're not here to own it or to keep parts of it or dig holes in it. When you go to Arnhem Land you know you're going over a piece of ground no one's ever walked across before. It's so friggin big. Nowhere else in the world like that except maybe in the Sahara desert. You walk around, sit on a rock under a tree and no other human has ever been there. They're just part of it. And it's a beautiful thing. And that's what you get with David.'

Hogan tells me he was going to use Gulpilil for *Crocodile Dundee 2* in 1988 but couldn't find him.

'And then I run into Ernie (Dingo), who's a mate of mine, and I thought, we can't have one Aboriginal in it who represents the whole nation so we had Ernie in the second one,' says Hogan. 'Otherwise it would've been David.'

Hogan lights a cigarette, a habit he kicked off sixty-four years ago when he was fifteen.

'Don't tell anyone. I'm always getting caught too,' he says. 'I was in the paper with Chevy Chase earlier this week and, sure enough, I was smoking. Chevy was smoking, too, but you didn't see the cigarette.'

I inspect the packet. I'm disappointed to find it's John Player & Sons (JPS), although when I turn the other packet over it's revealed to be Winfield.

'In the good ol' days when smoking was good for you and I launched Winfield, they were forty cents a packet! Now it's forty quid,' says Hogan. 'And it's all tax. They can make a packet of cigarettes like that for a dollar.'

Hogan asks me where David is and how he's doing.

I tell him he's being looked after by a wonderful woman in a country town on the Murray River near Adelaide, and that he's dying.

'Ah, shit,' says Hogan.

He leans back against the wall, draws on the JPS.

'Well, tell him I miss him and that I loved being with him.'

—— CHAPTER 9 ——

The Fanatic, The Follower and The Tracker

I T WAS A GIFT OF COINCIDENCE AND CIRCUMSTANCE that threw nineties heart-throb Gary Sweet into the unlovable role of homicidal cop and co-lead to Gulpilil in 2002's historical drama *The Tracker*.

The movie is set in 1922. We're deep in South Australia's outback. Gulpilil is a tracker ordered to find an Aboriginal man accused of murdering a white woman.

There are sparse introductions via titles.

No names.

Gulpilil walks while Sweet, whom we know only as The Fanatic, leads his two-man mounted troupe, which includes The Follower, a cop fresh out of training, and a grizzled man who is revealed as The Veteran. He's seen it all and, in the film's first major scene, takes repose with a cigarette while The Fanatic massacres a peaceful mob of Aboriginal men and women.

The movie pivots on Sweet and Gulpilil's relationship, each knowing the other or at least his sort, too well.

'In his most substantial role since *Walkabout*, top-billed Gulpilil is an extraordinary presence as the wise Aboriginal who quietly sets about subverting the expedition he's supposed to be guiding,' wrote the film critic David Stratton. 'With his expressive face and lithe body movements, the actor brings iconic status to the role.'

Stephen Holden of the *New York Times* wrote, 'Mr. Gulpilil has the mystical aura of a man so profoundly in touch with the earth that he is omniscient and safe from harm.'

Sweet was forty-three years old and shooting a guest spot on a kid's show at the South Australian Film School in 2000 when he stepped outside to smoke 'a bunger' near the office of the Dutch-Australian film writer-director Rolf de Heer. De Heer had carved a formidable reputation out of the bleak psychosis that was 1993's *Bad Boy Bubby*, winning both the jury and critic's prizes at that year's Venice Film Festival.

'I was probably looking a bit pensive, mulling over what relationship I'd just destroyed,' says Sweet now, 'and Rolf came out and saw me. I'd known Rolf for twenty years but we'd never really spoken. His opinion wasn't too high of me.'

Sweet, of course, was the actor whose sorcery on the television screen gave Australian women enormous pleasure every Thursday night when *Police Rescue* aired on the ABC. He'd won two silver Logies as most outstanding actor for his role as Sergeant Steve 'Mickey' McClintock and achieved minor success as a singer when his version of Billy Thorpe's 'Most People I Know (Think that I'm Crazy)' peaked at number fifty-two on the ARIA singles charts and lingered around the top one hundred for almost two months.

Sweet was gorgeous and popular, but too mainstream, you would think, for a director like de Heer, whose films were never designed for mass appeal.

'But he must've seen me in this different kinda light because when I went back to set there was a guy there I didn't recognise and he came up to me in a break in shooting and said, "Oh, look, would you have a moment to see Rolf?"

'Rolf and I, while we present differently, we discovered by doing this movie that we're very similar philosophically and politically and every other way. I was surprised and delighted to get the role. And that's when I met David.'

The filming took place over seven weeks, with a skeleton crew of fifteen, in Arkaroola, a wildlife sanctuary in South Australia's rugged, and stinking hot, Flinders Ranges, seven hundred kilometres north of Adelaide. Temperatures would regularly soar into the high forties, sometimes scratching even the mythical half-century.

'The second-oldest place on the planet, one point nine billion years old they reckon,' says Sweet. 'There was only one motel there and that was it. Nothing for miles and miles and miles. The only people that came through were, in the terms of the horse wranglers for the film, a bunch of German rock fondlers. We saw a lot of German rock fondlers.'

Sweet describes meeting Gulpilil as 'a life changing moment for myself. I'd never met anyone like him. I'd never met anyone so charismatic, so gifted. He could do anything. Absolutely anything. *Absolutely anything*. Ride a horse. Dance. Sing. Cook. I remember when I first saw him on *Walkabout*. He was riding a horse and I thought, wow, he looks like part of the horse. He doesn't look like he's sitting on the horse, he's sitting... *in*... the horse. His balance and his poise took my eye. His acting is intuitive and connected to country, so connected to the earth. He's mesmerising to watch. Not many actors have that and you can barely take your eyes off him. He's such a powerful presence but he's also hilarious, absolutely hilarious. He has very real emotions. When he laughs it's so infectious it's impossible not to laugh with him, even if you don't know the joke.'

Midway through the movie The Tracker refuses to continue until The Veteran, who has been speared in the side and has fallen behind, is allowed to catch up. The Fanatic whips and then shoots at The Tracker.

Still, he refuses to move.

The Fanatic: 'You'll stand trial when we get back. Disobeying orders in a field of conflict!'

The Tracker: 'Yes boss!'

The Fanatic, smiling: 'You'll probably... hang.'

The Tracker: 'Yes boss! Poor black fella. Been born for that noose, eh!'

The Fanatic, smile widening further: 'Too right.'

Gulpilil turns around and erupts in laughter. The pair dissolve into hysterics, Gulpilil doubling over.

'I can't help laughing when he laughs. He explodes with laughter and you get caught by the explosion and hit by the shrapnel. It's impossible not to laugh. It's my favourite scene. So bizarre. I mean, *"You're going to hang, yes boss, poor black fella, been born for that noose."* Quite a bizarre thing. Such poetry in the way it's told. It's poetry on screen,' says Sweet.

'There was both hell and heaven in that scene,' writes de Heer in his production diary.

When Gulpilil cries, which he does often and without shame, 'he cries like a child would. Disarming. Charming,' says Sweet.

When would he cry?

'Sometimes he'd cry if he reflected too much on the past or if he felt like he'd offended someone. His emotions are raw and aching with honesty. He reacts immediately to how he feels. When he cries, he looks like a cartoon crying, cries with his mouth wide open, a big *waaah* coming out of it. It's like he has no cloak. He lets his emotions out immediately and as an immediate response to whatever he's feeling at the time. He's a complex man.'

I ask Sweet if he noticed his hands, those strong levers forged in Gulparil, softened, and only slightly, by his Western experience.

'I used to love holding his hands. The first time I looked at his skin... it's beautiful... I'd never seen skin that colour, that gorgeous. He'd laugh at me when I stared at him. I wanted to touch him, hold his hand, be around him, feel the vibe he gave off. He was kinda tickled by it.'

Sweet says his co-lead as The Fanatic was a hard role to carry, emotionally as well as philosophically.

'It was profoundly difficult playing that guy although some people might say playing an arsehole comes naturally to me,' says Sweet. 'I had to get my head around the old fashioned noble savage bullshit to play that guy. I'd never heard such a load of crap, such a... such a... patriarchal load of crap from our white ancestors. It was so far from my own experience to play a character like that. It was almost surreal. I had no feeling at all. I'd get myself into such a state, a catatonic state where violence was just a way of life and that's how you dealt with it. The first time it was very difficult but then I got used to it and I'd slide into character when I'd get there. I had to abandon those fraternal feelings I had for David and get lost in the character. It's a horrible thing to do but I'd get rid of it from my mind, completely erase it after a day's filming otherwise it would've been too upsetting.'

In his production notes for *The Tracker*, director de Heer writes:

> Gary's first shot was awesome... he ranted and raved and railed at the chained Aboriginals like a true fanatic, powerful yet subtle, frightening whether or not you know that the real man is so far removed from the man he is portraying... I think the extras themselves understood what they were doing better than any of us could have explained it to them... they stood, captive in chains, and simply maintained their dignity through anything we could throw at them, any abuse we could visit upon them. David was the only one among us who was actually excited by the scene, by the nature of the depiction.

In his home country in Arnhem Land there are still people alive who were present at the massacres that took place there in the first half of the twentieth century, and for him to be seeing how some of it might have been was for him being in touch with his history. But it is our history too.

I ask Sweet for his take on white–black relations in Australia.

'My take is that it's the greatest disgrace in the history of Australian politics and I think that the whole thing's swept under the carpet, a forgotten problem. I don't know the answer. I don't know what to do. You know, we're always trying to make people like us, always trying to make people into ourselves whereas the Aboriginal race is nomadic. They don't want to stay in one spot. Why do they have to be like us? It's a conundrum that I haven't given enough thought due to my own laziness and shame for it. Who wants to be paternalistic? I did a series in Broome some years ago called *The Circuit* [a court-room drama set in the Western Australian town of Broome that ran from 2007 to 2010, employed a thousand Aboriginals as extras, and with Aboriginal actor Aaron Pedersen as the co-lead with Sweet] and it was only then that I fully understood the connection with Country. I remember going to a tribal meeting and we sat there on the red earth in Broome and I swear I could feel the heartbeat of the earth. That's when I realised that this connection to Country is a serious thing. It's just something that European folk don't seem to understand; it's a serious, serious thing.'

Gulpilil, says Sweet, spoke deeply of Country.

'He talked about his Country a lot. I never got to Arnhem Land to visit him. I wanted to. My life got in the way. I wanted to get up there when Rolf was making *Ten Canoes*. I would've loved to've gone up there. One night he cooked a meal for us, a kangaroo, and it was delicious. Magnificent. Of course it was! Unbelievable skills. He has an attachment to things that's... that's...' Sweet stutters, goes back over his words... 'It's difficult to put it into words. He's a very empathetic person. He *understands* Country. It was our last night when he cooked that dinner and I found it very emotional. I cried when I had to leave. I cried like a baby.'

Damon Gameau was a twenty-five-year-old actor two years out of NIDA when he won the role of The Follower, his first professional gig.

And it was a peach.

Sweet. Gulpilil. De Heer. Even the bloke who played The Veteran, Grant Page, was a dead-set Australian movie legend, a stunt man who'd doubled for Dennis Hopper in *Mad Dog Morgan*, falling backwards, and on fire, off a twenty-five-metre cliff.

'Anytime you get to do a job that has some historical truth to it, and *The Tracker* was based on diaries Rolf had found, and it doesn't feel like a vacuous production line job, you feel the integrity of it,' says Gameau.

The subject of Europeans massacring Aboriginals, with fervour and, mostly, impunity, has long been a subject of debate, framed as a left versus right issue. The so-called history wars.

In 2017, the University of Newcastle released stage one of its online map of colonial frontier massacres, 1788–1930, with this introduction:

> **From the moment the British invaded Australia in 1788 they encountered active resistance from the Aboriginal and Torres Strait Islander owners and custodians of the lands. In the frontier wars which continued until the 1960s massacres became a defining strategy to eradicate that resistance. As a result thousands of Aboriginal men women and children**

were killed... After 1930 the massacres continued but are not included here... This site is presented not as a conclusion but as a beginning.

To be counted as a colonial frontier massacre, according to the University, it must be the indiscriminate killing of six or more undefended people. Why six? The massacre of six undefended Aboriginal people from a hearth group of twenty people is known as a "fractal massacre". 'The sudden loss of more than thirty per cent of a hearth group leaves the survivors vulnerable to further attack, a greatly diminished ability to hunt food, or to reproduce the next generation or carry out ceremonial obligations to kin and country. In their diminished state, they also become vulnerable to exotic disease.'

Two hundred and fifty massacres meet the criteria of proof (Australian and British newspapers, missionary correspondence, explorers journals, shipping logs, government archival sources, Aboriginal accounts etc.), with six thousand two hundred Aboriginal and Torres Strait Islander people killed compared to fewer than a hundred colonists.

Says Gameau, 'You're recreating the attitudes of the day. And then you get a location like that where it... *breathes*. Mystical. Reverent. And we'd ride our horses to set and watch these spectacular sunrises and sunsets in very ancient country.'

When it came to performing alongside Gulpilil, Gameau says, 'Every actor tries hard not to act, to get a point where you're present. That's David. You never felt like it was a performance. He was completely unpredictable. Every scene, every take, was different. You look at him and something happens. It's a real trust thing. There's challenges. It's tricky and it can catch you off guard. But his level of talent comes with caveats. It's not all roses. Moments happen. You have to stand back, look out and go for the ride.'

Gameau thinks about it a little more, retrieves a satisfactory metaphor.

'It's like playing jazz. He doesn't know what it's like to do the same thing. It's different working like that. You can't keep to your own rote-learned performance. It's like playing techno with a jazz musician.'

Although he wasn't born when *Walkabout* hit theatres, Gameau saw it on TV as a kid and remembers being struck by Gulpilil's fluidity of movement.

'He's someone who can properly move and you can't help but be in awe of that. His grace and his ability to flow, that subtlety comes across in his dancing and his acting. He's like liquid.'

New to horses and roaming outback ranges, Gameau was anything but Gulpilil's liquid equal. On the first day of shooting, 28 February 2001, he had to strum a ukulele while sitting astride his horse. The noise spooked the animal, made it rear and threw Gameau onto a creek bed covered in fragments of sharp rocks. A sound transmitter strapped to his back prevented serious injury, although his pride was terribly wounded.

Gameau asked Sweet, 'Did I squeal before I hit the ground?'

'Some people move through space in an effortless way, a connection that's not fighting against anything,' says Gameau. 'They go with a natural grace. You see it in some surfers, a beautiful dancer, a great actor. When David walked across landscapes where you or I would clunk along heavily footed, tripping over rocks, he glided. In the West, we're linear and structured and it affects how you move and interact. Unlike David who is like mercury.'

The best moments of the shoot, says Gameau, were scenes shot from six kilometres away. Even with a giant 800-millimetre lens attached to the camera, the four actors were tiny as they traversed escarpments.

'For days we'd be riding on a mountain with no crew and they were the magic days. This is exactly what it would be like. No reminder of Western culture. No symbols of the modern world. Four guys on horses with an Aboriginal guy leading us. It was easy to suspend disbelief.'

Gulpilil and Gameau became close.

'He saw that I was open to learning the things he was willing to share. I hadn't experienced anything like that. When you're thrust into an environment like Arkaroola, you connect on a deep level. We'd sit around campfires and David would tell stories and share his wisdom and knowledge. It absolutely opened me up to another aspect of Australia. After the shoot, David asked me if I'd visit him at Ramingining and I jumped at the chance. It had a profound impact on me, to live with his family and hunt together, as I was developing my own views of the world. You see, you get this version of Aboriginal culture at school and [from] the media but it's not until you go to somewhere like Arnhem Land where you see how connected they are to the land, how important community is and their relationship to time and money. I remember seeing the impact of certain Western foods on the community and that inspired *That Sugar Film* [a documentary in which Gameau eats forty teaspoons of sugar a day to demonstrate the effect of hidden sugars]. There's a strong Indigenous element in that. And the visit gave me an environmental focus. About the nature of the land and how to care for it properly. It's stupid to ignore the wisdom of Aboriginal elders. I got that sense with David from the incredible amount of time they spend on the land, hunting and collecting and swimming in the waterholes. Then there was music, the ceremonies, and always being welcomed and how generous they were, sharing everything. It always remained with me.'

One year later at the Venice Film Festival, where the film would be given an Honourable Mention, Gameau was with

Gulpilil on the boat that delivered the stars to the northern sandbar stretch of Venice called The Lido, where the festival action took place.

Also on the boat was Italian film icon Sophia Loren.

'He had no idea who she was and he went up to her and was laying on the charm. I got to witness this extraordinary moment of these two people meeting each other for the first time.'

How did Loren react?

'She didn't know what to make of him. I wouldn't say she was overly comfortable with an arm around her in a confined space. But he was such a force of nature at that time. He's an infectious character with a playful nymph-like quality.'

Shortly before the boat tied up to The Lido dock, Gulpilil jumped atop the roof and started screaming, 'I'm Crocodile Dundee! I'm Crocodile Dundee!'

'The press went crazy. Ever the rock star,' says Gameau.

For the next five days, Gameau, Gulpilil and Sweet partied in Venice. A late-night swim in the green waters of the famous, and famously filthy, canals. Frequent nightclub visits.

'Whenever we crashed a dance floor he left a very strong impression. People gravitated towards him. He's such a free spirit,' says Gameau. 'Those film festivals are full of niceties and vanities and to have someone with such a disruptive nature, it's a joy to be around.'

Gameau last worked with Gulpilil in 2013 on the set of the semi-autobiographical *Charlie's Country*. Rolf de Heer has an enormous sense of loyalty to the people who help him make his films and, given this might be Gulpilil's last leading role in a film, and as it was probably going to serve as his legacy film, he employed previous co-stars in minor roles.

Sweet is a bottle shop attendant, hair shorn, and still with echoes of The Fanatic. Gameau plays a nurse in the Darwin hospital who tries to stop Gulpilil from walking out.

Still, Gulpilil was more than a fellow actor.

'Every time I went to Darwin I'd have some sort of catch-up with him. The last time I saw him was in 2016. He hadn't been diagnosed and he was very much in terrific spirits. He'd given up booze, pot, he was in a bright space. We had a beautiful connection. I still feel a strong sense of love for that man. The things he showed me, this very young and naive twenty-five-year-old, shaped my life.'

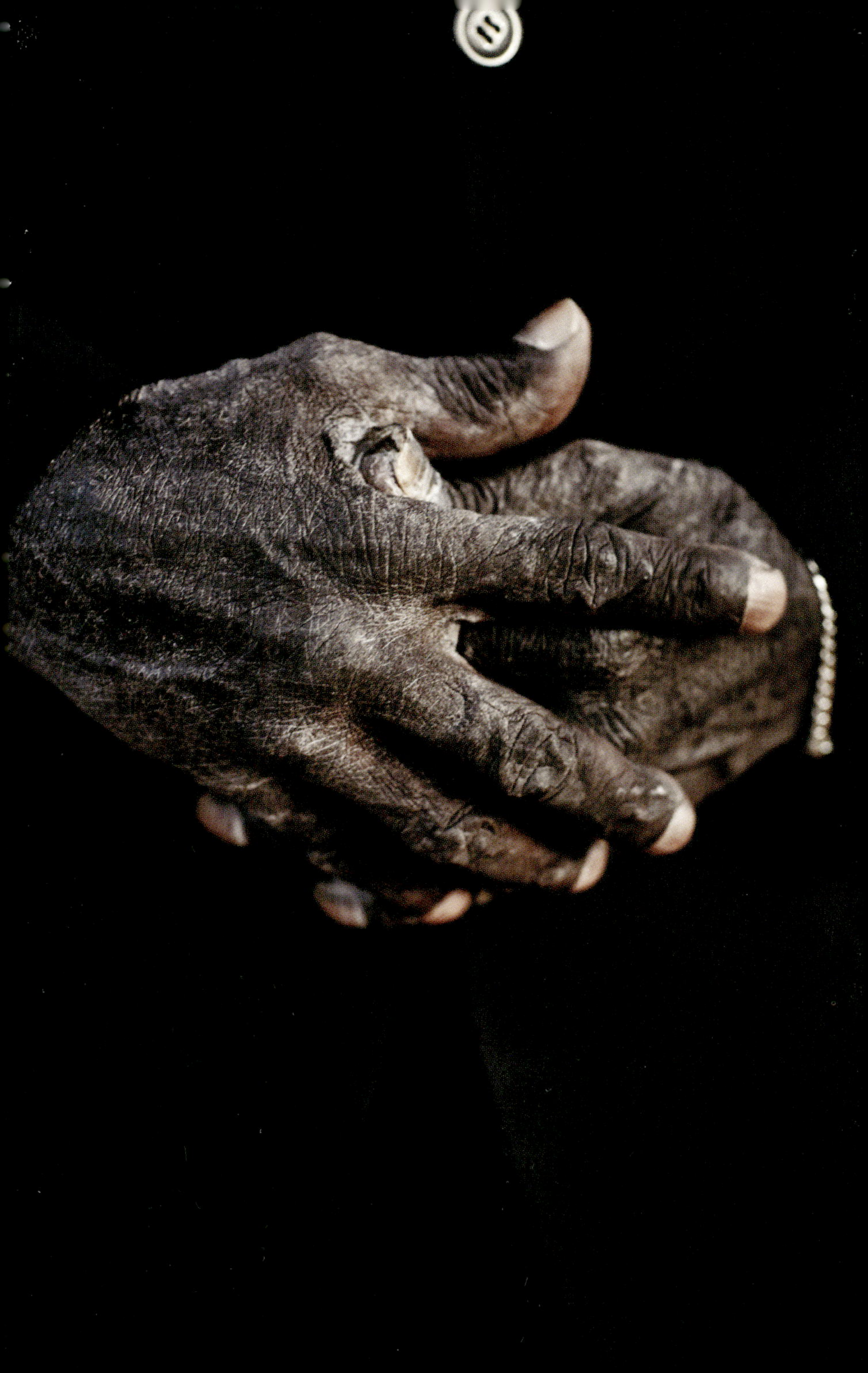

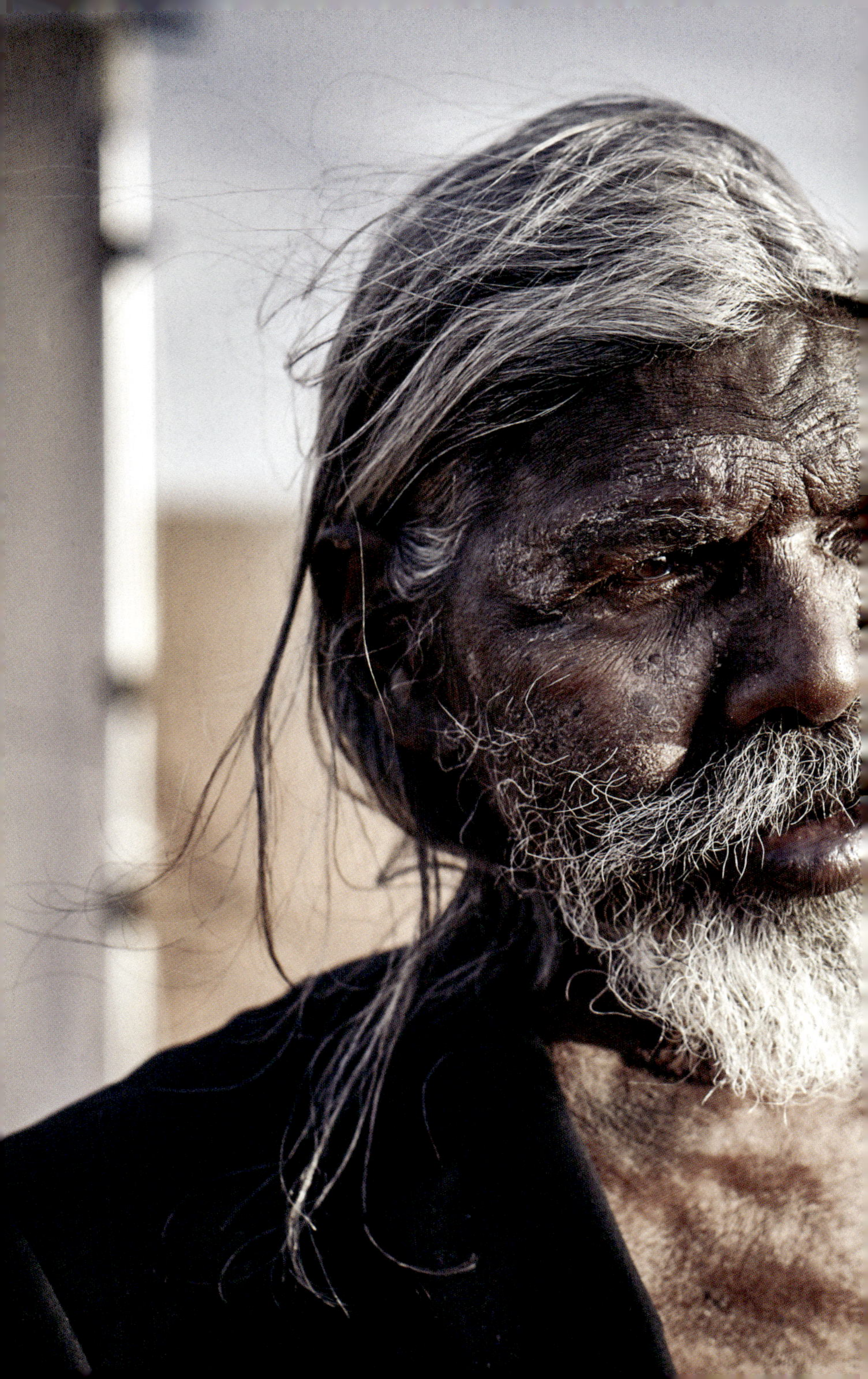

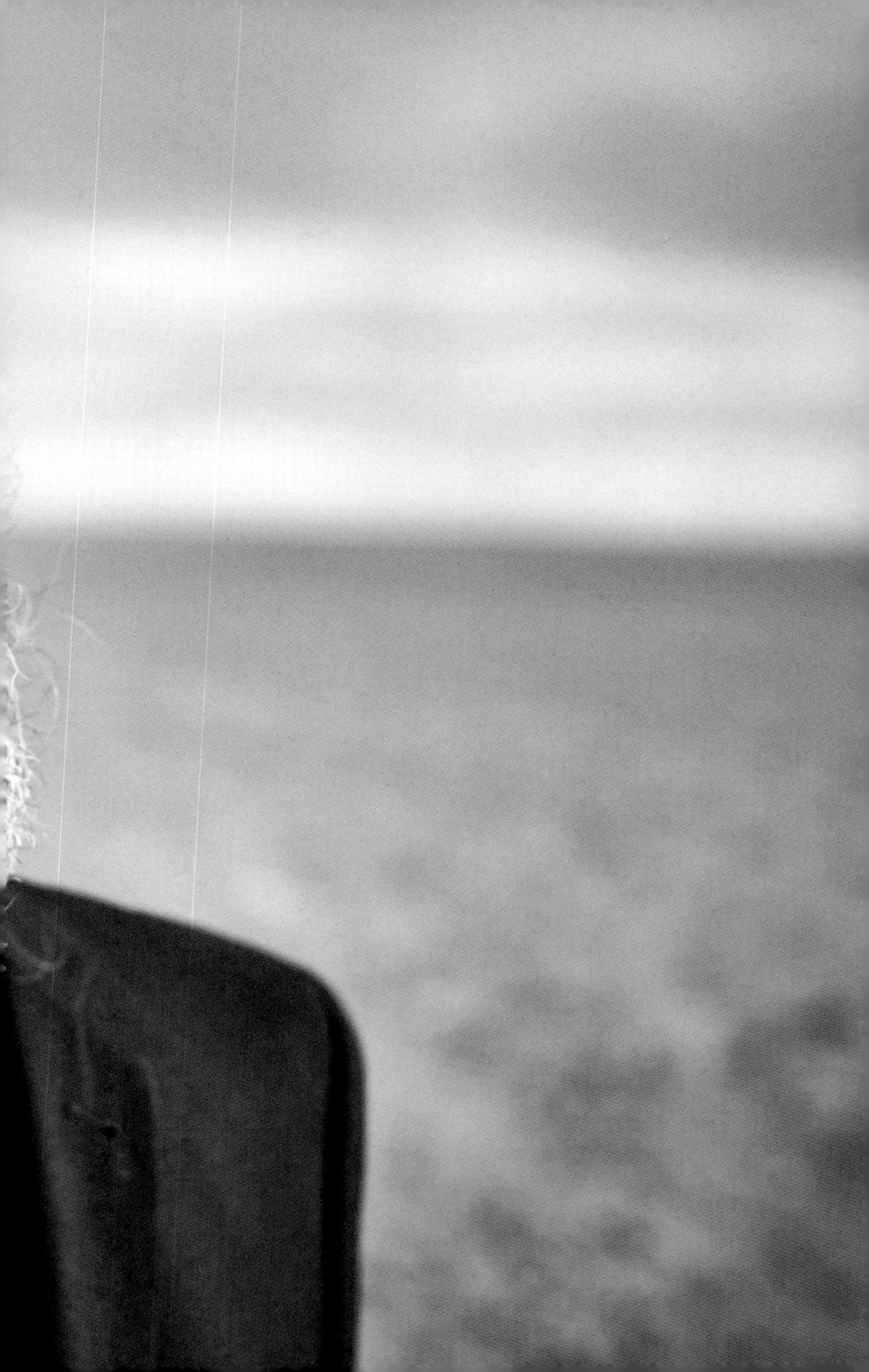

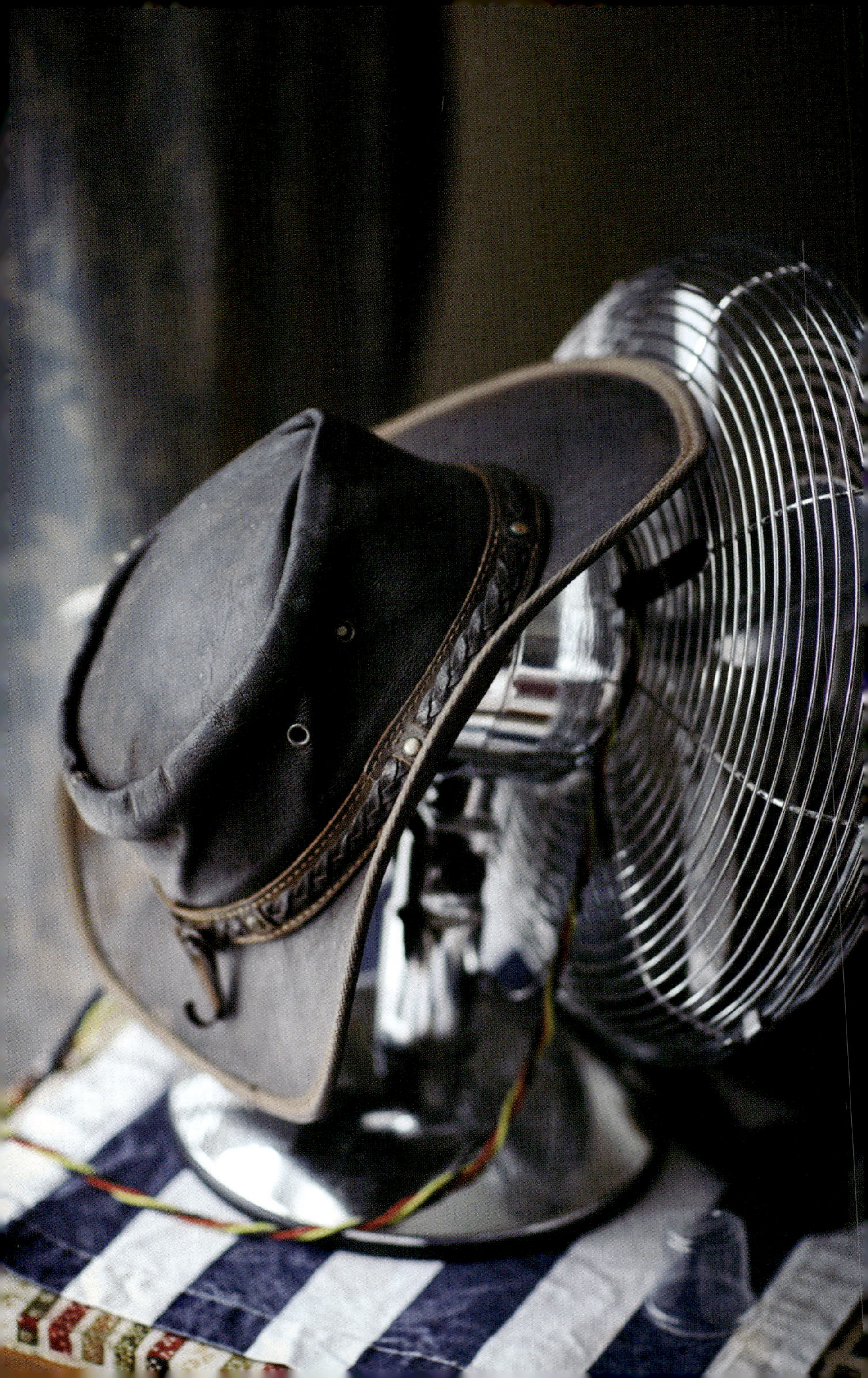

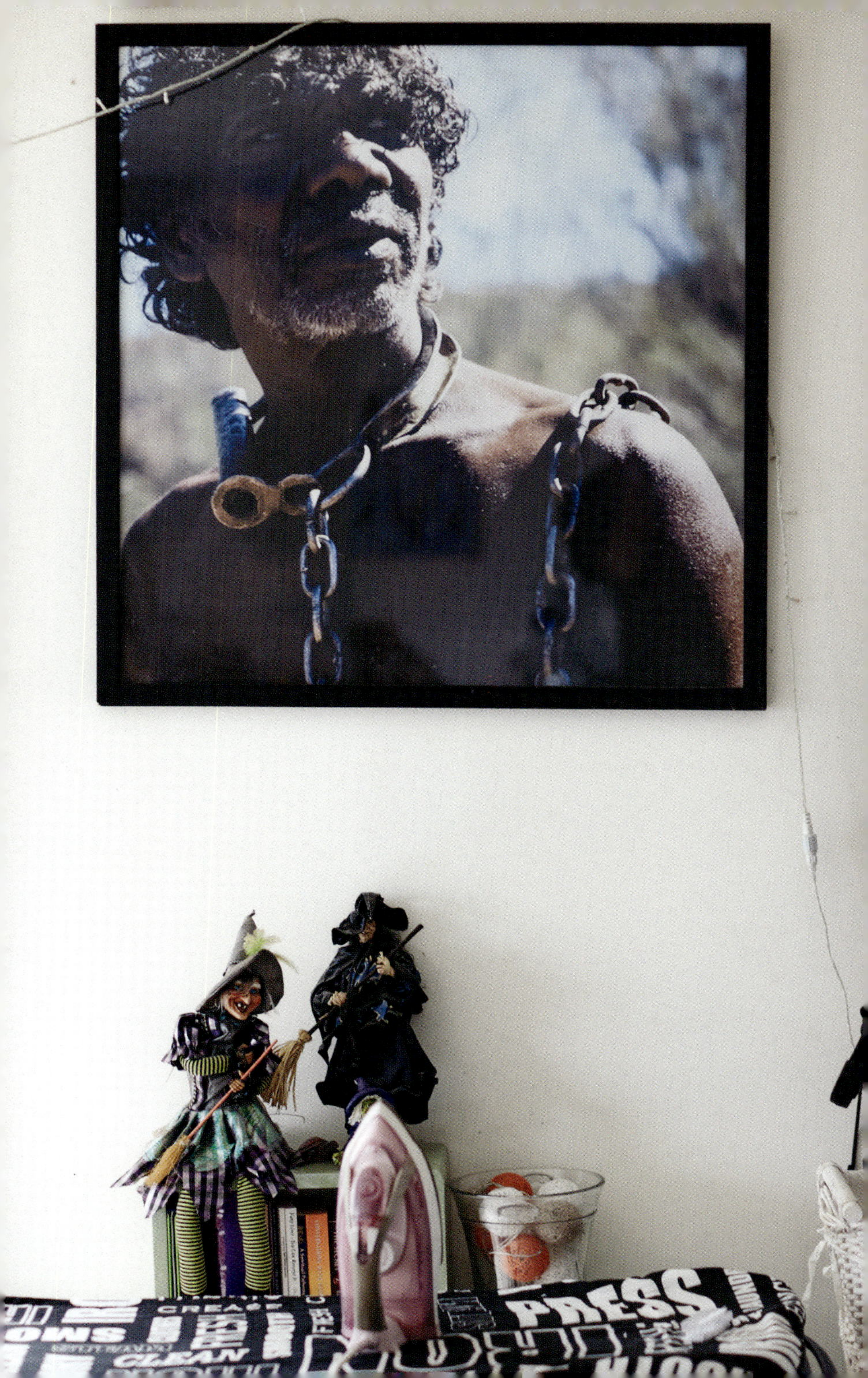
PRESS
CLEAN

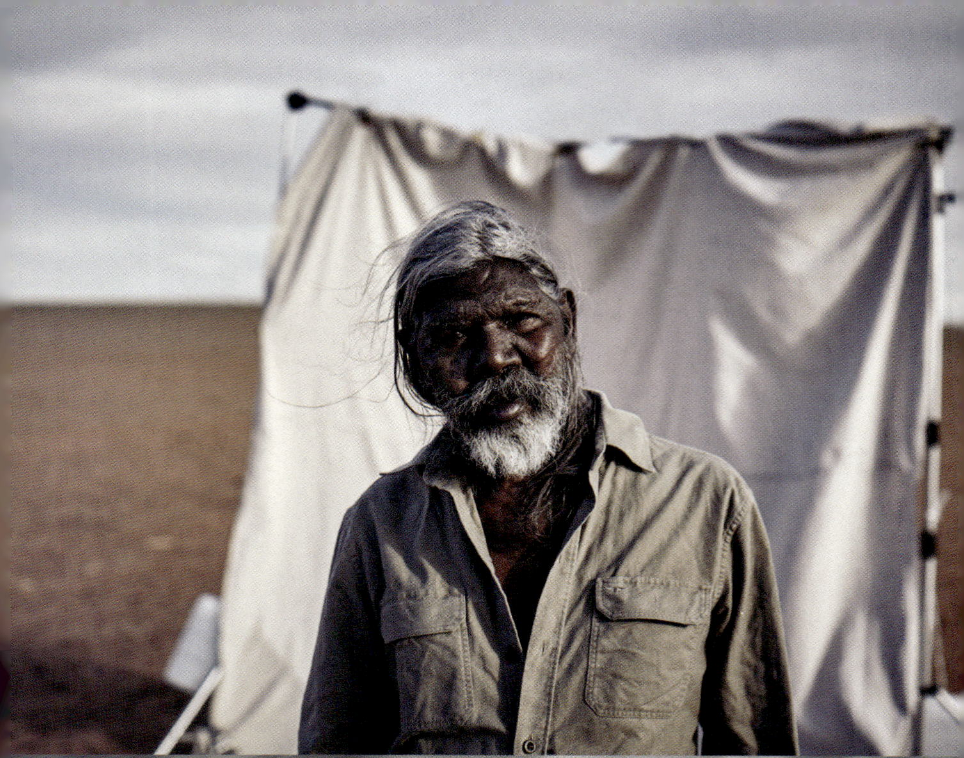

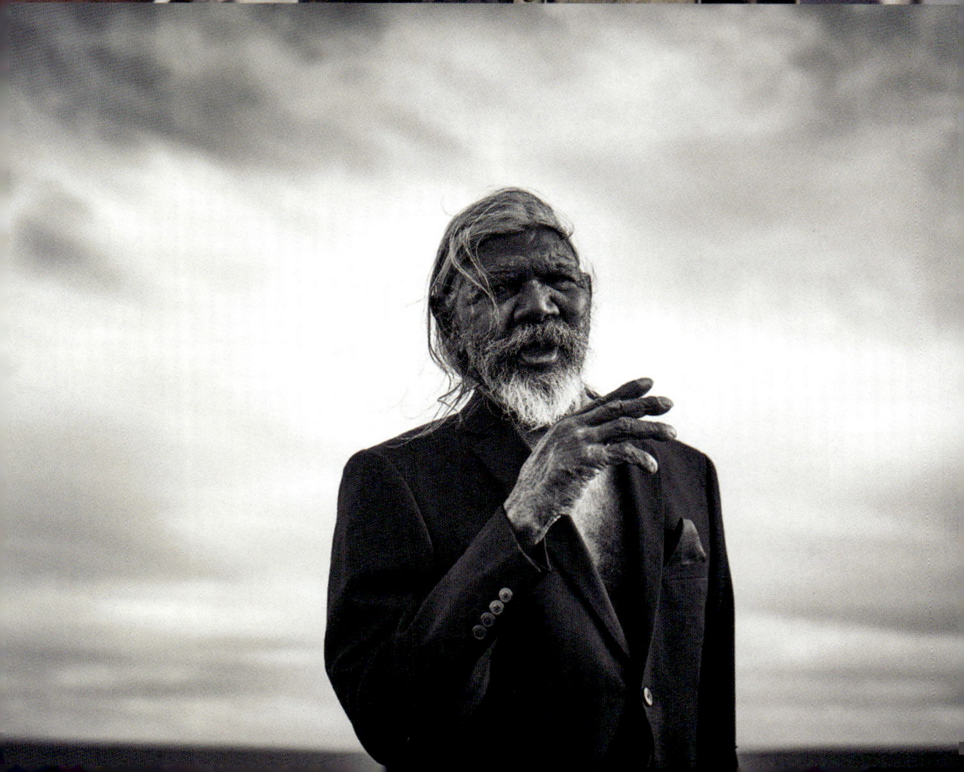

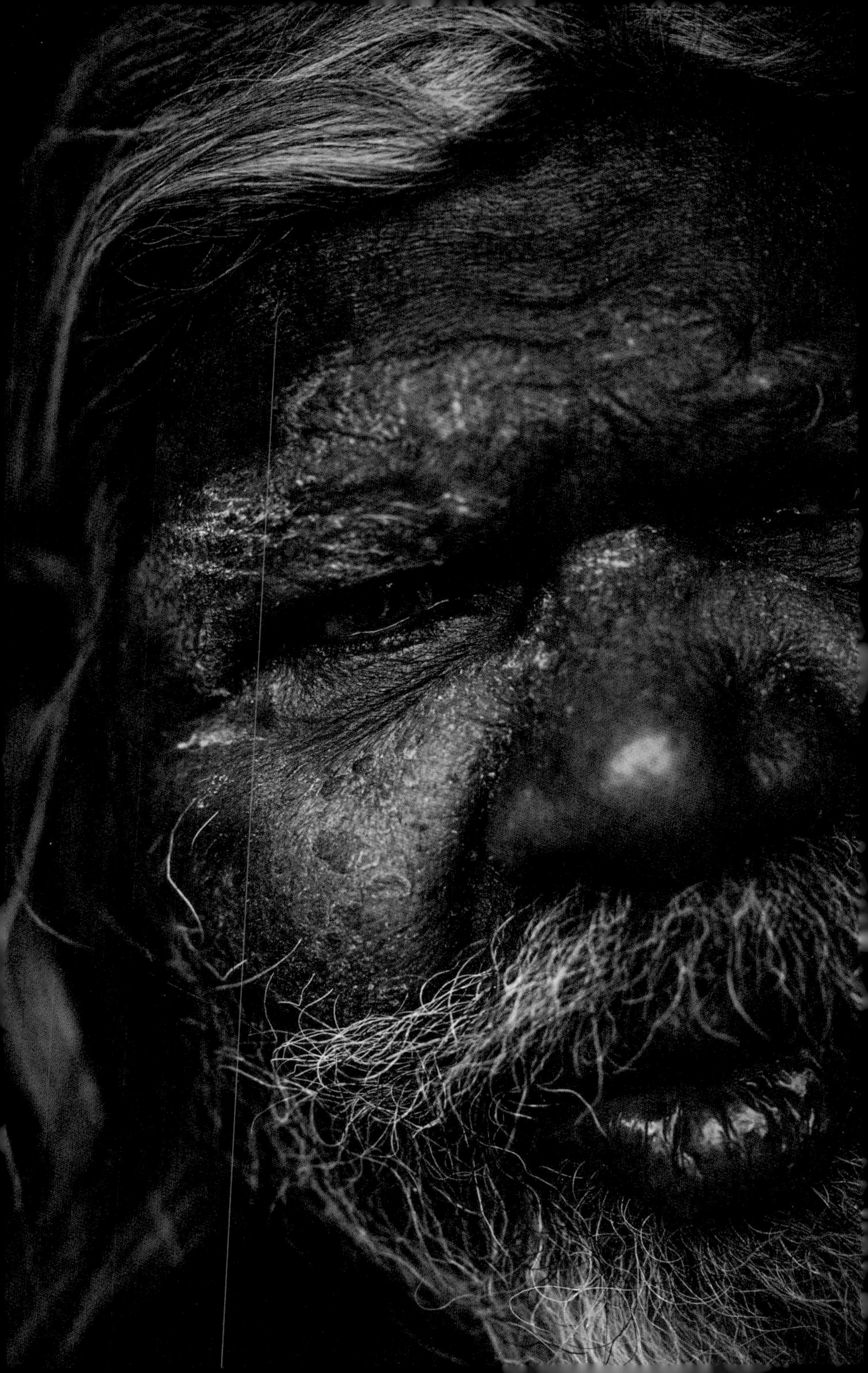

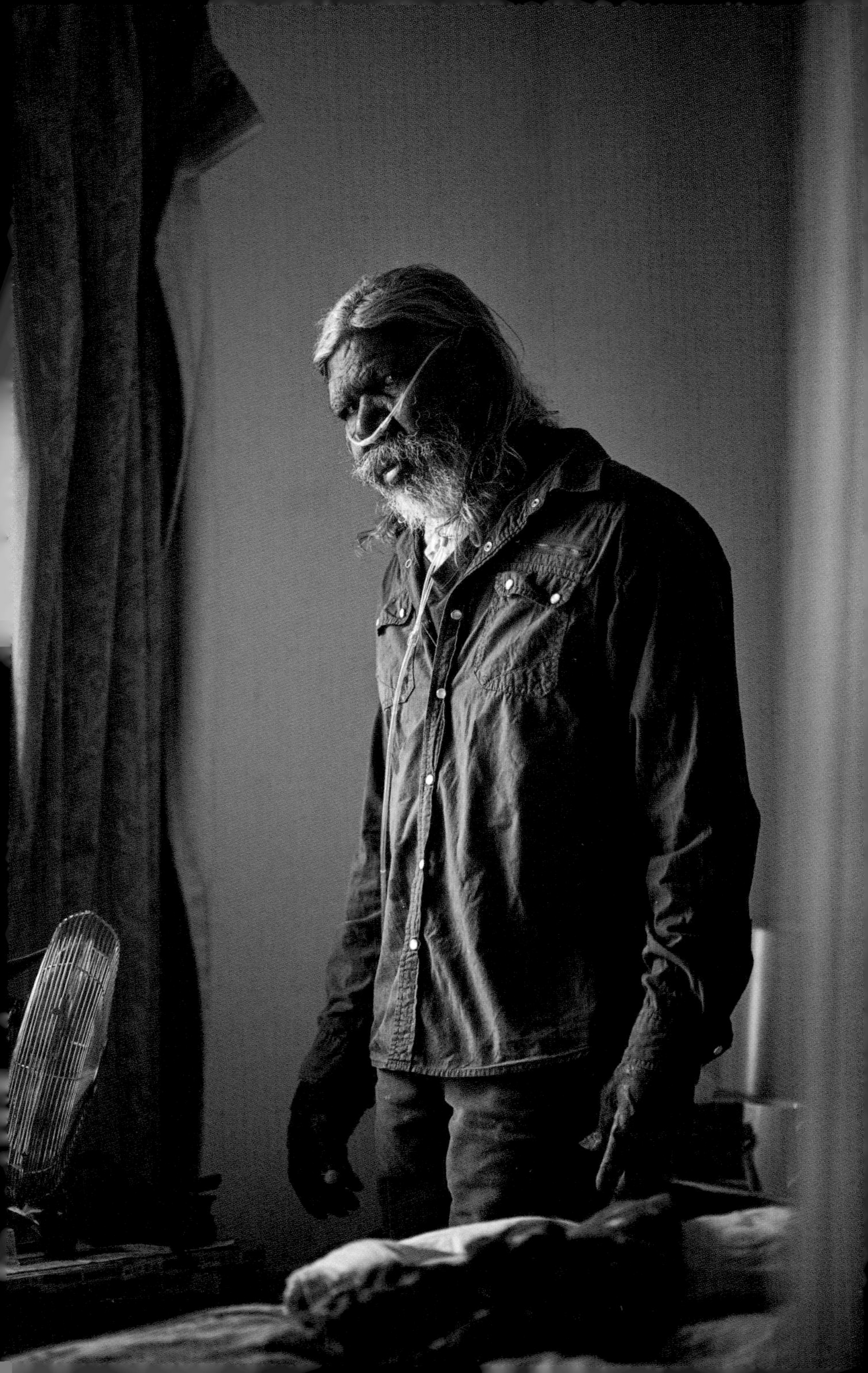

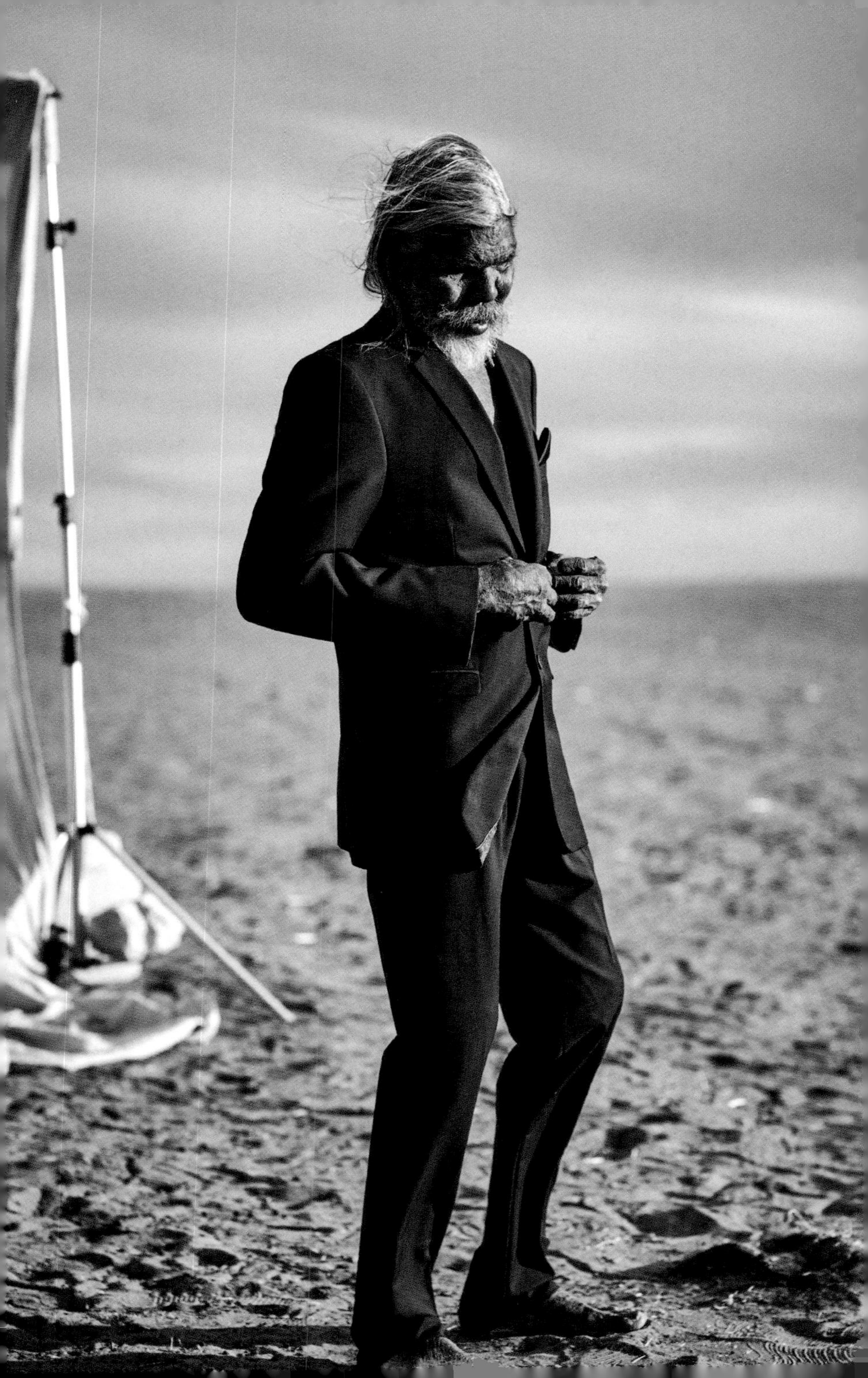

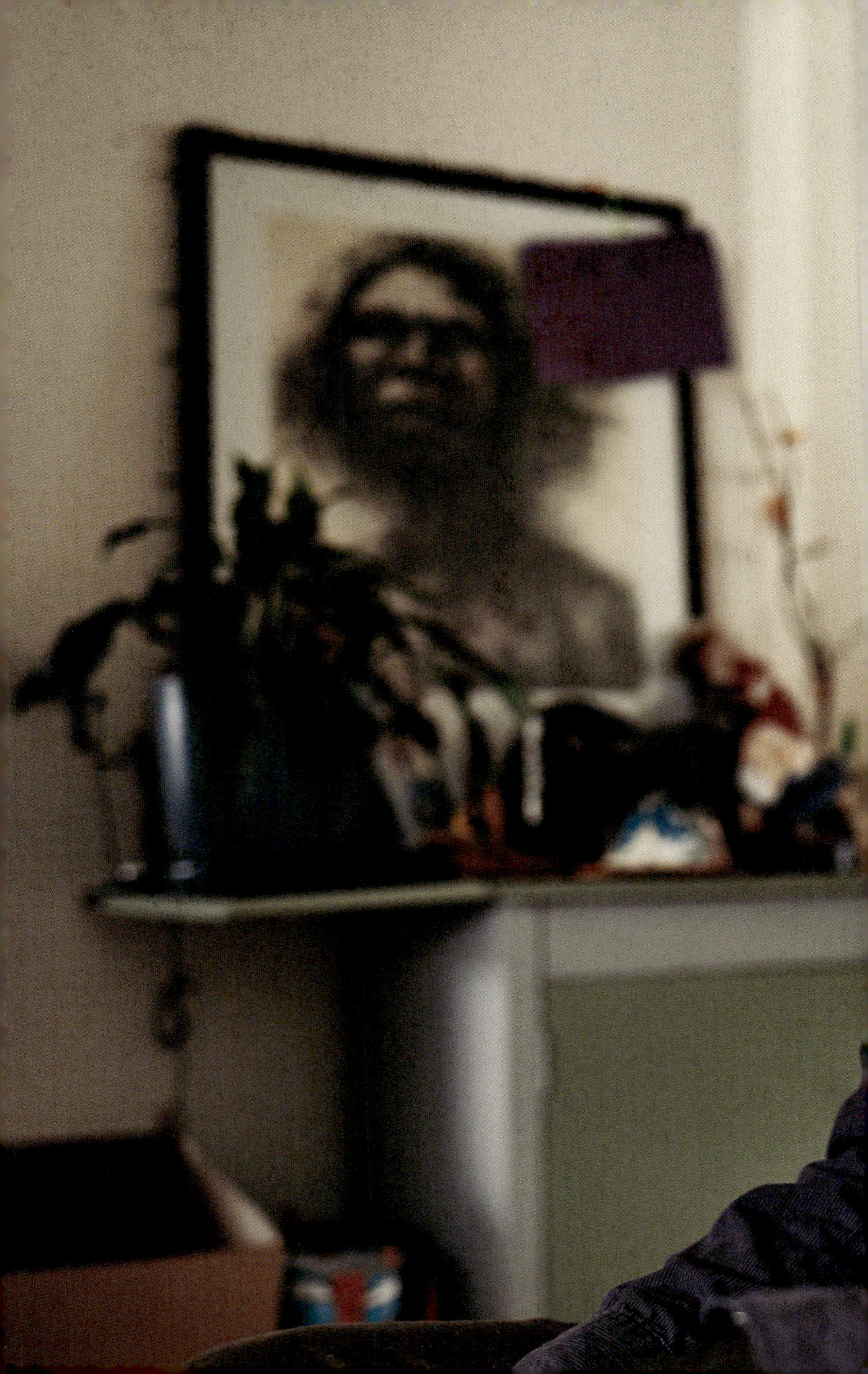

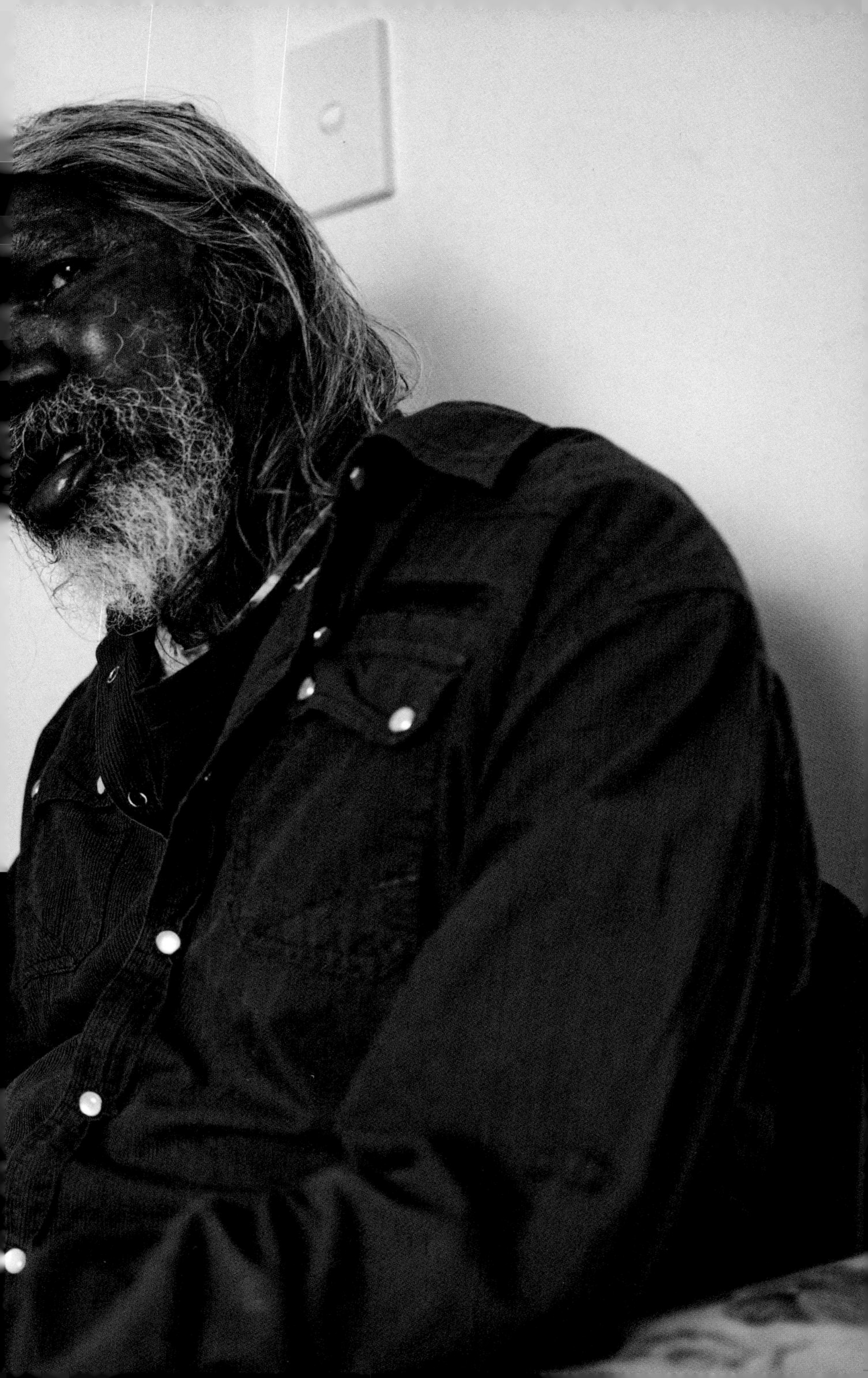

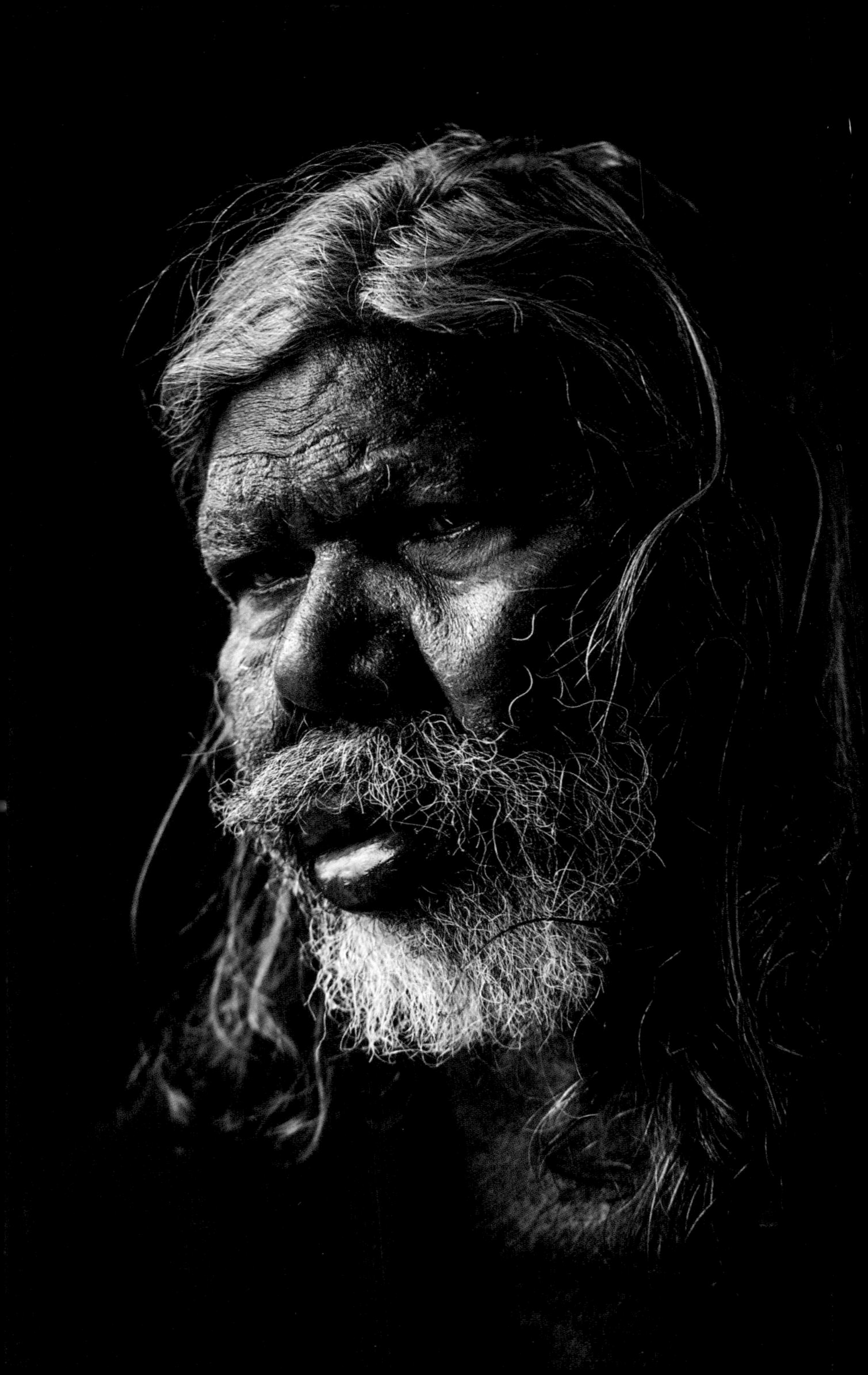

CHAPTER 10

Gulpilil: The One-Man Show

F OR TWO WEEKS IN MARCH 2004, GULPILIL, ALONE on stage, sold out the 620-seat capacity Dunstan Playhouse at the Adelaide Festival.

Dressed in a tuxedo, with a white shirt unbuttoned to reveal the topography of his crocodile hunter's torso, Gulpilil played out the tragicomedy of his life, from dancing tribal boy to movie star who is feted by Queen Elizabeth II, to prisoner in Darwin's Berrimah jail. The adoring audience responded with a standing ovation every night.

The set comprised a fire, a corrugated iron humpy and a large screen that showed clips from his movies, *Walkabout*, *Storm Boy*, *Crocodile Dundee*, *Rabbit-Proof Fence* and *The Tracker*.

If Gulpilil stumbled on his words, or hit a blank, he would prod the fire with a stick which would alert the stage manager to whisper his lines into an earpiece, hidden behind his long hair.

After somewhere between ninety minutes and two hours, depending on his vibe on the night, the fifty-year-old would climb down from the stage and shake the hand of every single audience member.

'I'll never forget the opening night. He was dynamic. You could tell it was huge to get his story up there. You couldn't take your eyes off him,' says Reg Cribb, who wrote *Gulpilil* at the request of Bangarra Dance Theatre's head Stephen Page, who was also the artistic director of the Adelaide Festival.

As Page explained in 2004:

> I thought about this strange, Hollywood kind of world in which he lived in one part of his life, and the cultural responsibilities of the world in which he lived back home and in that sort of mysterious, powerful stillness on the screen I would see the struggles of the two worlds in him ... and I thought that this would be ideal material for the stage.

Page had been turned on to Cribb's ability to write strong Indigenous leads with his play *Last Cab to Darwin*, about voluntary euthanasia and set in the Northern Territory.

Later plays with Indigenous themes would include *Krakouer!*, about footballers Phil and Jimmy Krakouer, and *Country Song*, with the performer Jimmy Little.

Gulpilil was a co-production with Belvoir Street Theatre's Company B and directed by Neil Armfield, who would make the Heath Ledger, Geoffrey Rush, Abbie Cornish film *Candy* in 2006.

Of course, masterworks like *Gulpilil* rarely come easy.

'I knew it was going to be the most challenging thing I would ever do,' says Cribb. 'And of course it turned out that way. It was a very, very tricky process.'

In an interview shortly after the play's release, he told the reporter of a Sunday newspaper magazine, 'It's been a battle ... There's a lot of suspicion from David about white people. He doesn't realise that with this play he can own something artistically for the first time.'

To gather material for the play, Cribb was flown to meet and work with David for three weeks at his home in Ramingining. He was met at the little airport by Gulpilil, his wife at the time and various kids running around.

'So much of his life has been recorded in newspaper articles and film work and interviews, but you want to get into who he is and what his life is,' says Cribb. 'Even though I was raised in wheatbelt WA and I'm used to small places I'd never been on solely traditional land. The spirit and the heart of the place didn't reveal itself until I'd been there a few days. You realise you're a guest and there's certain parts that you're not privy to. David would be up all night, painted, doing ceremony. I'd sit around the fire with 'em at night but once it got into ceremony I had to make sure I wasn't around. David would have nights where he had no sleep at all. The next day he'd be bright and bushy-tailed. He was fifty and he still looked like a god! Six-pack abs! Strong! One day, the cops needed him. There'd been an attack on one of the white teachers, female, and they called David in to track. I watched him do his thing. He studied the leaves and the trees and the ground and somehow tracked the guy responsible. He is a ... *real* ... tracker.'

For the movie star veteran, life wasn't as simple as it might've immediately seemed to the outsider.

'You could never tell who was David's friend and who wasn't,' says Cribb. 'There was always stuff going on. There was a bit of conflict and jealousy between people in the town and him, and what he does, one foot in the white world, one foot in the black world. He's always crying poor. He'll come in and he'll give away all the money he made on a film, sometimes pretty good money. He'll give it all away. And everyone expected him to.'

Gulpilil gave Cribb a tour of his humpy, an expansive construction made of corrugated iron and with tarpaulins draped across the roof and held down with poles of stringybark trees, the same eucalyptus used to make canoes.

He showed his AFI awards. A crocodile skull. His Don Dunstan Award for lifetime achievement in the arts.

'My mate Don Dunstan,' muses Gulpilil in the show. 'Years ago when I was goin' to film and TV school right here in Adelaide and he was Premier of South Australia, I was livin' close to the same street as him. He invite me and my wife over for dinner and play the piano. He make music for me to say welcome. And there was this Russian fella there. He was a... ballet man. What was his name? Nureyev! Anyway... I'm playin' in this theatre now. The Don Dunstan Playhouse. He was a top fella. Thank you, Don. Hard to find fellas like him any more in the top jobs. That feels like a long time ago now.'

As tour guide for Cribb in his humpy at Ramingining, Gulpilil laughed. He danced.

'I wasn't getting a lot out of him but once he started doing his comedy routines, and he's such a natural comedian, I thought this show's gotta tap into those skills, as a lot of them [Aboriginals] have. We tend not to use that aspect of their characters.'

If you'll allow a slightly out-of-the-box, but important, diversion, we might examine a speech Tony Abbott made at the annual Reconciliation Australia Dinner at Old Parliament House in 2014.

> We Australians underestimate the contribution that Indigenous people have made to our national ethos; the stoicism, the laconic humour, and the endurance that has come to characterise us as a nation. I doubt it came ashore in 1788 because, frankly, it doesn't characterise the English, the Irish or the Scots but it came to characterise Australians... and that humour which is now very much our ethos, indeed a part of our soul.

Real Aussie humour! Direct from Arnhem Land, brother.

Says Cribb: 'Gulpilil wanted to be a movie star, he wanted to be Mel Gibson, he didn't necessarily want to play the noble savage.'

In a later aside, Cribb says Gulpilil told him about an upcoming role in the movie *Australia* with Hugh Jackman and Nicole Kidman.

'"Baz Luhrmann wanted to pay me money to stand on one leg, I'll do that! I can play the token black fella!"

'So once we tapped into that humour, the stories started coming out. We decided to have him on stage and start the story as if we're inviting them onto his boat for a journey down the Glyde River to hunt crocodiles.'

Cribb had his own taste of crocodile hunting on the Glyde with Gulpilil. Before making the two-hour trip, for which they'd depart Ramingining at 11 pm, Gulpilil had ripped the roof off his old blue LandCruiser so they'd have a lovely open-air ride to the river.

A photo of Cribb and Gulpilil shows the pair in front of the four-wheel-drive, each holding one horn of a water buffalo skull mounted to the bumper bar. Cribb has the soft middle belt of the white fella writer, contained beneath matching navy blue polo and shorts. Gulpilil wears only tiny denim shorts, which are strapped onto his waist by a leather belt, the sort that are now the preserve of female Instagram influencers. His body looks as if a surgical vacuum has removed every millilitre of adipose tissue.

All the way to the Glyde, Cribb kept asking Gulpilil, 'Are you sure you've got enough fuel for the boat? Are you sure? I've got all this money from the Australia Council. We can fill up.'

Gulpilil waved him away, 'Nah, nah, all good, brother.'

They arrived at the Glyde at 1 am, set up camp and then launched the little aluminium runabout. Cribb piloted the boat while Gulpilil, now in a lap-lap, stood on the bow with a harpoon.

Cribb said he couldn't see the crocs.

Gulpilil told him, 'You're not looking hard enough! You can see all the little red dots! There's thousands of the bastards everywhere!'

Once spotted, Cribb would kill the engine, they'd float by the doomed animal, Gulpilil would spear it through the brain, roll it up in rope, pull it to the side of the boat and go to shore.

Around 3 am, the boat ran out of fuel.

Cribb and Gulpilil were two hours walk from their camp and the four-wheel-drive.

'What do we do?' asked Cribb.

'Walk!' hooted Gulpilil, looking up at the full moon.

'And David just left me and walked off,' says Cribb. 'I was walking through this swamp, sinking up to my waist, I can hear crocodiles scuttling into the water, I keep bumping into water buffaloes. It was the most terrifying two hours of my life.'

When Cribb made it back to camp, Gulpilil had his head in a bucket bong.

'I couldn't help it, I'd been so good up to that stage,' says Cribb, 'and I let fly, "I fucking told you to put fuel in the thing! Why didn't you listen to me? I nearly died out there! There's a lot of stories for which I'll bleed to write but I'm not going to fucking die to tell it."'

Gulpilil smiled beatifically.

'Now you're ready to tell my story...'

After a period of back-and-forthing between Cribb and the director Neil Armfield, a draft was realised. The next step was to get Gulpilil down from Arnhem Land and into Sydney for rehearsals.

'With David we knew we had to keep him away from temptation,' says Cribb. 'So instead of rehearsing in Newtown, we took him down to his agent John Cann's property on the Colo River (near Windsor in Sydney's northwest), where we spent four weeks rehearsing the show.'

The actor and musician Terry Serio, who played the title role in the television production *Shout! The Story of Johnny O'Keefe*, among dozens of other significant film and TV roles, was brought in to manage Gulpilil.

'I had drug and alcohol problems, drug problems for a long time, so when David was doing his one-man show John Cann asked me how would I feel about being David's wrangler,' says Serio, now sixty-three. 'You can't bullshit a bullshitter if you know what I mean.'

During rehearsals, Serio would buy Gulpilil light beer.

'This beer makes me ... *sick*,' his charge would complain.

Roll of eyes.

'It *does*, brother, it *does*, brother!'

Serio told him: 'What do you want to do? Do you want this job or do you just not want to do it? It's as simple as that!'

His own experience with Indigenous Australians was formed as a kid growing up in Western Australia. Serio remembers driving to Bindi Bindi, population seventy-two, with his dad, who'd served in World War II. There were soldier settlement farms there; a total of 1095 of 'em were spread over thirty-six thousand square kilometres in WA, which meant the family could move from nearby Wongan Hills to have their own piece of dirt to farm.

'My dad mentioned there were black guys in the war, up in Borneo with him, and I suddenly made the connection: Did they get the soldier settlement farms as well? Dad looked at me and said, and my nickname was Tige, "Tige, when they got back from the war they got nothin'." I asked him why and he said, "That's just the way it was." I could see it broke his heart. I could see he could not rail against it, he could not go against a system that was so firmly in place. I could see the anger and hurt it caused him. And that blew my mind. To see the power of the white culture that would silence someone as passionate as my dad.

And then somehow silence me as well. It just was so weird to know that the white people came back from the same war and got all these benefits and black people got nothing.

'One of the things that struck me about Gulpy was how hurt he was. How hurt he was by the fact that he was given so much but also given so little. He was this guy in our midst that was like a warrior, and at the same time an artist and, at the same time, reviled and loved. How do you live with that dichotomy, that mixture...'

'At one stage,' says Cribb, 'we thought he's not going to be able to remember his lines and they'll have me asking questions, interview-style. Neil was very frustrated. I was very frustrated. Neil was clashing with David. There was this tension between David and Neil and I was in the middle. One time, Neil lay in the river and started to float down the stream. He wanted to float away. It was the hardest thing he'd ever done.

'But this was David's story. He wanted to tell it. He wanted everyone to know the real story. It was never easy for this traditional man from Ramingining to operate in a Western construct of the entertainment industry.'

In an interview three days before opening night, Armfield told a reporter, 'When he is away from his country, he is unstable. The connection is religious for him. The land is not just territory, it is his self. When you are off your land, you are no longer yourself.'

'It was a complicated thing to wrangle Gulpy because he needed a lot of wrangling,' says Serio, 'His whole idea of a work day was completely different to anyone else's. There'd be times where you'd be working through script stuff, trying to work out what was going into the script, but he'd be thinking about something else: food, or beer or worried whether he was going to have enough beer to get through. It was a strangely complex thing. You couldn't get to a point where you were telling him what to do because that wouldn't work. You had to cajole and encourage and give him lots of pats on the back and be a little bit firm on occasion. He'd go into a funk really easily ... It was crazy to work with.'

In the show, Gulpilil talks about the difficulties, which can't help but be comedic, of connecting his tribal existence with the demands of a Western movie set.

'One day, about eleven years ago, I'm sittin' here in Ramingining, mindin' my own business, and my agent in Sydney sends me a fax.

'It say: "David! They want you! You gotta be in Melbourne in two days for a part in *Man From Snowy River*."

'And I'm thinkin' shit! Melbourne ... two days? No worries. So I gotta drive over to my Father's land at Gulparil, 'cause my personal assistant Wayne was livin' rough out there. So I jump in my vehicle. A Toyota LandCruiser with two plastic seats and that's about all. It's just a chassis with wheels. I call it the "never-ending story" 'cause it just keeps goin'. So I'm driving through the swamp for hours and, you know, it's the wet season. When I get there, Wayne says: "Where we goin' David?" and I say "Melbourne. Jump in!"

'So then we're goin' back through the swamp and fuck me ... cough ... cough ... splutter ... we run outta petrol! No worries, we walkin'. How far ya reckon, Wayne? Oh, eighteen hours. No worries. So we trudgin' through the swamp and saltwater river and dodgin' crocs. Eighteen hours later we walk back into Ramingining and we charter a plane to Gove on the East coast of Arnhem Land. We get to Gove but we just missed our connecting flight to Cairns. So I gotta hire a charter flight to get to Cairns. And on the way to Cairns the spirits whipped up a big wind ... *whoooosh* ... and all hell breaks loose!

'We just manage to dodge the cyclone on the way and get to Cairns. But our plane to Melbourne is taking off. Stop the bloody plane! So we jump out and take off our knives and bullets and bush tools 'cause we flyin' Qantas now! And we both look like Swamp mob 'cause we still covered in mud and shit from walkin' home. So we on the plane to Melbourne and then we get there and I say "Hi, Man from Snowy River! I'm here!"

"'Hey, David. Glad you made it. We don't need you for three days 'cause the shooting has been delayed."

'And you know what I made for that job? $5000.

'You know what it cost me to charter a plane to Cairns? $5000.'

Late one night after rehearsals, Cribb, Serio and Gulpilil were sitting around by the river. Gulpilil announced that he wanted to go into town for a drink.

'We thought we'd humour him,' says Cribb. 'It was after 10 pm, nothing open. So we go into town and nothing is open. David rolls his window down, calls someone over and says, "I'm Crocodile Dundee, you must know me!" The guy goes, "Yeah, yeah, I think I recognise you." David asks where he can get a drink. The guy tells him to go to Richmond. So he insists we drive him to Richmond. We find a karaoke bar. David gets on stage and starts acting out the show at the karaoke bar. Everyone knew who he was but no one knew what he was doing.'

As his wrangler, Serio had a lot of down time with Gulpilil in this old wooden house on the river. Silence. Reflection. Talk. It's how you get to know a man. The pauses that stop being pregnant. The knowing glances. The ability to gradually peel thoughts open over days, weeks.

'That's when all the stuff would come out about the difference between black and white and there being no difference at all,' says Serio. 'It broke my heart when I first heard the line "one red blood" because I thought, fuck, it's so... *yes*... every time when we start hammering Muslims or whatever, you look at the colour of the blood. And what's different? We had these long conversations about where you fitted in to the world. In his stories, in the sense he made, he felt that he was on the outer, no matter what, 'cause he couldn't make sense of anything that was happening to him. It's a terrible cycle, feeling the pain, trying to numb the pain. That started very early on, from the time he first started working in the film industry. The pain that came from him was extraordinary. I'd go, "Fuck, no wonder you drink!"'

I ask Serio how he could feel Gulpilil's pain.

'How would it present itself to me? I'd see him holding back tears. I'd see his eyes glass over and talk about how he was lost. I think he could feel himself falling between the cracks of those two worlds, the black and the white world. There were times I thought, here's a guy who has so much to offer us yet no one wants to know. Part of it is he's a black guy who drinks a lot, but no one would give him a chance. Maybe the reason he drinks a lot is because no one is listening to him! I don't know what that is like for a black person in Australia that knows that the country that says they love you actually doesn't in their heart. I don't know what that does to you.'

Being on the Colo, says Serio, did give Gulpilil a little peace.

'It was a very special thing for him to be in a place that he felt connected to. All of the things that we take for granted or don't even see, he could see. Like, animals, insects, whatever. He was alive. He was part of the environment. We forget, because of how we are, that we are always removed from the environment we're in. We build houses as far away from the natural world as possible. We try to keep nature waaaaay out of it. Black fellas aren't like that. They know we're part of this. And let's face it. If you can walk through some of that country where he lived, fucking full of crocodiles and snakes, most of us would be terrified. But it's nothing to him. He's part of it. He's not walking *around* it. He hasn't got boots on. He doesn't have the armour. He understands it.'

After the Adelaide Festival, *Gulpilil* went on to sell out theatres in Brisbane and Sydney.

In Adelaide, once the hands had been shaken on opening night, Gulpilil grabbed Reg Cribb and told him, 'You the writer, you always knew what was going on. I love you, man.'

Cribb smiled, wryly.

'I love you, too,' he told Gulpilil, 'but you're a pain in the arse, mate.'

CHAPTER 11

As Moodoo in Rabbit-Proof Fence

THE DIRECTOR PHILLIP NOYCE IS ONE WEEK BACK in Hollywood, from the Kolkata International Film Festival, where Indian audiences thrilled to a retrospective of his films, including *Clear and Present Danger* (Harrison Ford), *Patriot Games* (Ford, again), *Dead Calm* (Nicole Kidman), *The Quiet American* (Michael Caine) and *Salt* (Angelina Jolie).

The centrepiece of the retrospective was the Stolen Generations film, *Rabbit-Proof Fence*. Gulpilil stars as Moodoo, an Aboriginal tracker whose job is to find escaped Aboriginal kids from the infamous Moore River Native Settlement in Western Australia, a camp for so-called 'half-castes' forcibly taken from their families and interned, and whose own daughter is imprisoned there.

On the day of the Kolkata screening, Noyce was surprised to see the cinema encircled by lines of people. By the time he was introduced on stage, every seat was taken and people stood in the aisles.

'Standing room only and they weren't going to see some Bollywood film,' says Noyce.

The film is based, loosely at times, on the 1996 book *Follow the Rabbit-Proof Fence* by Doris Pilkington, whose mother, aunt and cousin are the film's protagonists, Molly, Daisy and Gracie.

Two of the three girls successfully navigated the twenty-four-hundred-kilometre, nine-week trek back to Jigalong, from where they had been taken in 1931. Doris also spent eight years at Moore River, where she trained as a nurse and later worked in Aboriginal health before turning to journalism.

'Mum would probably never have told me the story,' Doris said at the film's 2002 premiere at Jigalong. 'She never tells me much, except what she thinks I should know. I used to believe she handed us over to the government. I even accused her. We were living at Geraldton at the time, and we brought her down for Christmas, and I said to her, "Why did you give us away?" And she just broke down and cried and said, "I didn't give you away. The government took you away from me."'

In Kolkata, when Molly and Daisy successfully make it home, the crowd cheered the house down. Confirmation, if any was necessary, perhaps, of White Australia's wicked, racist past.

The film's scriptwriter, Christine Olsen, was spurred into bidding for the script rights in 1996 after reading a seventeen-hundred-word feature about the book that appeared in the *Sydney Morning Herald* called 'The Long Walk Home'. Olsen, a documentary-maker by trade, spent three years making repeated visits to Jigalong, as well as collaborating with a script editor, before realising what it really needed was a director to breathe life into it.

Olsen obsessively pursued Phillip Noyce, the influential Australian director now based in Hollywood, because of a little-known film he'd made in 1977 called *Backroads*.

The fifty-seven-minute film, 'a short feature', which was made using sixteen-millimetre film, starred Bill Hunter and the Aboriginal activist Gary Foley, who agreed to appear in the film only if he was given control over the film's Indigenous voice.

'Gary said he didn't want any part of white man's bullshit unless he got to monitor all of the black content,' said Noyce, who would later gift the film rights to Foley. 'So we reached this agreement that he could rewrite his dialogue whenever he thought it was bullshit; he could have a say in the movie's content.'

Hunter and Foley play two drifters who steal a 1962 Pontiac Parisienne and commit a series of crimes before the inevitable bloody showdown with police. A simple enough premise, except the driving scenes are punctuated with dialogue about race relations.

'[Noyce] treated the Aboriginal people as people, nothing more, nothing less,' said Olsen.

After various cold-calls and an ultimatum to make the film or she'd take it elsewhere, Olsen eventually landed her target and Noyce made the film in 2001 for a 2002 release. *Rabbit-Proof Fence* was a critical and box-office success. Made for $US6 million, it took $US16 million worldwide at the box office.

'... it's an extraordinary piece of storytelling by Phillip Noyce and his team,' says the film critic Paul Byrnes. 'Within a few years of its coming out, an enormous number of Australians had seen this movie – far more than had watched any previous Australian film dealing with an Aboriginal issue.'

The American critic Roger Ebert wrote:

> The final scene of the film contains an appearance and a revelation of astonishing emotional power; not since the last shots of Schindler's List have I been so overcome with the realization that real people, in recent historical times, had to undergo such inhumanity.

In a story in the conservative literary journal *Quadrant*, Keith Windschuttle, whose work includes the multi-volume *The Fabrication of Aboriginal History* and *The Breakup of Australia: The Real Agenda Behind Aboriginal Recognition*, wrote a ten-point rebuttal of the film called 'Holes in the Rabbit-Proof Fence'.

'Many school teachers think it is an accurate portrayal of history,' writes Windschuttle. 'It is anything but. The film gets the names of the major characters and locations right, but not much else. It is a work of dramatic fiction that tells at least ten major falsehoods.'

Not that the film is an obvious polemic.

'Noyce's sensitive dramatization swaps angry politics for emotional sympathy,' wrote the BBC's Jamie Russell, 'concentrating on the plight of the children instead of ranting against the authorities'.

And Gulpilil, as Moodoo, the conflicted tracker, is central to the depth of the film.

Noyce says he had wanted to work with Gulpilil ever since he first saw him in *Walkabout*.

'To see David upon that screen was a revelation,' says Noyce. 'Back in the sixties we were still unaware of the treasure trove of diamonds that we had in our country. We were in the Middle Ages, the dark ages, the blind ages, in terms of appreciating what our Indigenous culture had to offer us and the world. And David was one of those people that opened Australian eyes and opens the eyes of people all around the world to the splendour of Indigenous culture.'

Noyce cites the tennis player Evonne Goolagong and the boxer Lionel Rose, 'but they were all excelling in white man's pursuits, whereas David, well he was excelling in cinema but he was celebrating the uniqueness of Indigenous Australia. And that was stunning to see'.

Two years after *Walkabout* hit cinemas, the dozen students at the newly established Australian Film and Television School, in Sydney, which included the then twenty-three-year-old

Noyce, were told a thirteenth student was coming to join 'em. Gulpilil.

'And David came in and, as we've seen for centuries, and as we've seen in white-and-black relations in Australia, everyone tried to tell him what he wanted to do. He came to learn to be a filmmaker but instead the film school used him almost as a guinea pig. They went out to make a film about him (called *Showing Melbourne to Maningrida*) which they shot. He sort of appeared in the movie but it wasn't really his movie although it was meant to be.'

The pair became close. Gulpilil stayed with Noyce and his then-wife Jan Chapman at their house in Annandale.

'And the man that I got to know was a little overwhelmed of everything that had happened to him,' says Noyce. 'Because [*Walkabout* director] Nic Roeg had found him up in the north and taken him all around the world. David was catapulted into the upper echelon of government, arts and royalty all around the world, lionised. And at this point [in 1973] he was coming back down to earth in a way. Finding his feet.'

Gulpilil was at the school, on and off, for three months.

'A lot of that time was spent back up in his home country making the film that was meant to be his training as a filmmaker,' says Noyce, 'but in a sense, it was the very well intentioned staff at the film school using him as a subject for a film. It reminded me of a documentary [*Another Country*, 2015], which he had a lot more authorship with, where it's very much David's point of view about what's gone wrong in two hundred years of interaction between white and black Australia... David's question is, why didn't you ask us what we wanted? Because we would've given a good answer and we wouldn't have this mess we have now. It's full of his incredible insight and wit, his ability to see things from white, black, the past, the present and the future all at once. And it's full of pithy Gulpilil humour.'

Two years passed before the pair saw each other again. Gulpilil was shooting *Mad Dog Morgan* in rural Victoria and Noyce followed the shoot just to watch him act.

'And he was having the time of his life!' laughs Noyce, 'David's a... *rake*! This young man. You've never seen another person like him, or as charismatic, with the *unique* charisma he has. Because every movement. His humour. His intelligence, *searing intelligence*. His... his... good humour. He's always had an incredible good humour. He can always defuse any situation with a smile, with a movement of his arms, his fingers, or just a few words.'

Another two years apart followed and, again, Noyce went to watch Gulpilil act, this time on the set of Peter Weir's *The Last Wave*, set in Sydney but shot in Adelaide because it was riding on the back of funding by the South Australian Film Corporation.

'I went to the set of each of these movies so I could watch him work and marvel at the way he commanded a scene, any scene, without doing much...'

Noyce thunder claps with laughter.

'... Or doing *a lot* with equal force.'

'Finally,' says Noyce, 'with *Rabbit-Proof Fence* I got to say action and cut with David. Finally, I had the pleasure of working with him. And he is one of the most talented...' Noyce, stops, then booms, 'IF NOT... *THE*... MOST TALENTED ACTOR I've ever worked with. And there's been some good ones.'

Noyce isn't exaggerating, He's worked with Harrison Ford, Michael Caine, Willem Dafoe, Richard Harris and James Earl Jones.

'You can't compare him to anyone else. He's in a league of his own,' says Noyce. 'Because he's playing those characters who have only enjoyed, well not enjoyed, a relationship with White Australia for much less time than people you see on a cinema screen. He belongs to the past, in that sense. Because of the way in which Australia was colonised, and conquered of course, there's some two hundred years difference between contact on the east coast and contact in the north. Up to two hundred years difference. And David was lucky enough...'

Noyce laughs at the absurdity of Gulpilil's supposed luck before correcting himself.

'*We*... are lucky enough that he was born into a world that was largely untouched. He is one of the great links with sixty thousand years of Australian history because he grew up traditionally. Because he knows about the sun, the moon, the stars, the Milky Way. He knows about the animals. He knows and he understands and transmits all the beauty of Indigenous Australian culture, its practises, its history. And he carries that with him with... *huge*... dignity into every role that he's played. We're lucky that Nic [Roeg] found him. *He's* probably not lucky that Nic found him. Although maybe he is, because maybe it gave him the power, strength and the opportunity to [not only] be himself, but to be all these other characters, and to see so much more of the world.'

But, says Noyce, 'From Bennelong to David, there's a long history, a long tragic history of interaction between white and black. And, you know, Bennelong, like David, was celebrated for his beauty, for his charm, for his athleticism and he too was taken across to England and met the king and the queen and was applauded. While when I think of David I think of all the positive things, I can't help but think of the negative things too. And I don't think negative things for us, but for him... Being born when he was, he was never going to be able to be the undiluted David that Nicolas Roeg found for the rest of his life. And yet, he's been so many things to all of us. It's a bittersweet relationship.'

In *Rabbit-Proof Fence*, the three Aboriginal girls in the film were cast after Noyce travelled to Indigenous communities across Australia trying to find the perfect blend of authenticity and on-screen presence. Kids were photographed with up to five cameras rolling simultaneously, Noyce says, to see how 'self-aware' they might be under the pressure of filming a six-million-dollar movie.

None of the girls had acted before.

'David came just before we started shooting and our lead actress [Everlyn Sampi], who was twelve at the time, was having a lot of trouble settling into the role, settling into playing someone else, settling into the discipline that was needed to work a rigorous schedule. She was feeling dislocated because she was away from Broome for the first time.'

Noyce asked Gulpilil to 'put some magic' on the young actress.

'And he stepped in and really connected with Everlyn Sampi in ways I could never have done. And then the real pleasure started. David had read the script and he understood the character [Moodoo] so well. I didn't need to tell him . . . *much*. You stand over there, you come here, you're looking at her, that was about it. The performance in the film was all *his*. And, he would always absolutely define the drama of the moment. He would absolutely etch, brilliantly, the emotions of the character.'

Gulpilil owned the character to such an extent that Noyce rewrote a pivotal scene at his insistence.

'He does something that is so representative, I'm sure, of a lot of interactions with white Australians. And that's where he's hunting these three girls. He clearly sees evidence that they're nearby. And, he looks down, sees their footprint, and then, all in the one shot, rises and tells us, with the most subtle movement of his eyes and face, that he knows exactly where they are, but, for his own good, for their good, for everyone's good, he's not going to say a word about it. And yet he's been tracking them for twelve hundred miles! He's finally found them and now, as a recognition of what they need to do, and what he needs to do as a forceful political statement, he frees them right under the nose of his white police boss. He lets them go.'

The original script had Moodoo losing their trail.

During the shoot, Noyce could sense Gulpilil's reticence at playing the scene. He told the director, 'I can find these kids, I can find them anywhere. It's so easy.'

Noyce told Gulpilil that, for the sake of the story, he *couldn't* catch the kids.

'I could see that he was frustrated,' says Noyce. 'I tried to demonstrate to him how they could avoid him but he just wouldn't accept it. But once again, he agreed, he acquiesced to my power, and then as we were shooting a scene where he's looking down at maybe the children's tracks, I suddenly realised what David was trying to tell me. If he can't catch them, then he doesn't want to catch them.'

Noyce laughs.

'And it was all his own work! The shot, the look, I didn't say or do anything. We turned the camera on him and he did it. It didn't need any explanation to him. He didn't need any preparation. Actors prepare themselves by training, by getting to know a character, by perfecting an accent, by perfecting a body language. Well, it was the opposite with David. It always was. He didn't have to act. He just had to . . . *be*. And, not that he wasn't a great actor, I'm not saying that, it's just that each of the characters that he played was inside him already. And he just had to let them come out. And the job of the director was to capture that, each of those characters. He is a living national treasure. Like some other extraordinary Australians: Sidney Nolan, Cathy Freeman, Don Bradman. I put him up there. I put him right up there with Don Bradman. He's an icon.'

Another scene in the film shows Moodoo riding his horse through the Moore River Native Settlement. He sees the three girls. They return his gaze. His expression is immovable.

What does Moodoo's look tell the girls? That he's watching them? That he feels for them?

'This is David's gift,' says Noyce. 'His acting style could never be confused with acting. *Ha!* And his looks were always precise in all of his parts, but while he's acting a particular emotion he also turns his face into a mirror. So that you look at him and, combined with his own expression and his own emotion, you see what you want to see. You know, I've looked at that gesture that he gives to those girls on the porch outside the baby's nursery. And sometimes I see a face that's stern and warning. And other times I see a face that recognises potential. And he's actually encouraging them. I've watched the film thousands of times. Literally. And I watched it again last week in Kolkata, India. And I saw something completely different in that gesture. David's face really is a mirror. It allows your own emotions to ricochet off it. And that's real acting. That's what a truly great actor does. They multiply the possibilities of response in the audience. David always did that.'

Noyce quietens. 'How is he? He's hanging on?'

I say Mary found him in the shower without a pulse just before my visit a few weeks earlier.

'She, what? Oh dear.'

Noyce asks, 'Shouldn't he be back up in the north? He doesn't want to get trapped down in South Australia. He should be back up there. Being down south is a little bit . . . [exhales] I don't know if it's the right spirits down there. He's a long way from home, you know. But . . . maybe, maybe that's a good thing. I don't know. I'd say if they want him to get better they should send him back up north. It's a bloody cold place, Adelaide.'

I tell Noyce it ain't that easy. Gulpilil isn't immune to the fear of being removed from the medical support he trusts in Adelaide. And there's his ongoing dislike of plane travel. And the pressure of returning to his community, the money that needs to be shared, the pressure, the pressure.

Ever the director, Noyce becomes lost in a sort of reverie about his great friend, a man he's known for forty-five years, that he has admired for almost fifty.

'His face . . . his *face*,' he says. 'His face just has *so much power*. He's a living national treasure who is a link to sixty thousand years of Australian history and culture. We are lucky. He is a living legend.'

CHAPTER 12

Battle of the Ancestors

T**HE ACTOR NATASHA WANGANEEN HAD JUST** turned sixteen when she was cast in the role of Nina, the hard-edged dormitory boss to Gulpilil's tracker Moodoo, in *Rabbit-Proof Fence*.

'I was a child when I met Uncle David and he overwhelmed me,' she says, juggling a kid and conversations with various family members on a bus to Port Adelaide, where she lives.

'There are things that change you and people that change you. When I saw him I saw the strength of our men and the strength of our culture, the strength of storytelling and the strength of taking a chance. We don't see fellas like him walking around with their chest out and looking straight at you. Normally, everyone's trying to ignore you. When he stares at you, it cuts through your soul.'

Wanganeen's role in *Rabbit-Proof Fence* wasn't a stretch for the teenager to play. She was born at the one-hundred-and-fifty-year-old Point Pearce Mission on South Australia's Yorke Peninsula, which, before the arrival of the European pastoralist in the mid-nineteenth century, was the land of the Narungga people.

The four clans that made up the Narungga, the Kurnara (north), Windera (east), Wari, (west) and Dilpa (south), were displaced as pastoral leases ate up their country, their hunting grounds and their water holes, which stretched from Port Broughton in the north to Port Wakefield in the east and all the way down to the Yorke Peninsula. Six-and-a-half thousand square kilometres of tribal land.

Throw in disease, a belief among some Europeans that Aboriginal people were barely human and therefore could be despatched with impunity, paternalistic law and the introduction of rabbits, camels, goats, cats, foxes and donkeys, which trampled the native vegetation and destroyed much of the Aboriginals' food supply, and the subjection was complete.

The *Aborigines (Training of Children) Act* of 1923 meant Aboriginal kids could be forcibly removed from their parents at the whim of 'The Chief Protector' and sent to institutions until they were adults.

This practice continued until 1963.

'One of the oldest missions in Australia, one of the scariest,' Wanganeen says of Point Pearce. 'Growing up there, a lot of ghosts, spirits. When I tell black fellas from interstate where I'm from they say, "Point Pearce? Oh my god, that place is . . . *scary*."'

One day, on the Mission's television set, Wanganeen saw Gulpilil as Fingerbone Bill in *Storm Boy*.

The impact was immediate and profound.

'I looked at him and said, he's like me, I'm like him. And it made me feel good. It made me feel happy and proud. When I looked at him, he let me know I had a place here. That it's a part of us, we're here! It's such a beautiful thing to do to an Aboriginal child when you grow up on a Christian mission. Watching him be so happy and free and such a larrikin. That's exactly us!'

Wanganeen adds, 'I never thought I'd get into acting, by the way.'

Less than a year before catching *Rabbit-Proof Fence* director Phillip Noyce's eye, she'd joined her Aunty Josie Agius's Port Youth Theatre Workshop.

When it came to the audition for the film, 'It was like, "Crap, this is an audition, what am I going to do?" I just started acting silly and I got the part,' she said in 2004.

On that first day on set, Wanganeen was hit by terrible nerves, her heart shuttlecocking in her chest, legs playing an internal vibrato. She says she felt like she had just stepped into the orbit of a black superhero.

Gulpilil looked at her calmly, stood up and asked, 'Are you okay?' Wanganeen replied with a tremulous, 'Yep.'

'I didn't say anything else, just stood with him,' she says. 'I just got this feeling from him. I didn't have to say nothing. You don't realise how much power he's got until you're in front of him. He's spiritually and culturally strong. You can't fight it. You just let it happen.'

Noyce talks about the 'magic' Gulpilil put on the film's lead, Everlyn Sampi, who plays Molly, and I tell Wanganeen how he soothed her feelings of dislocation at leaving her hometown for the first time and explained how the whole acting thing worked, and how she could shine.

Wanganeen saw it, too, and says that Gulpilil recognised himself in Everlyn.

'She was untrained, fresh in the game, another beautiful kid, a Noongar kid, very strong in her culture and her language. She had the same power that he had when he was like that. He didn't push her. He walked with her instead of in front of her. He does that a lot. He sees the quality of that person and if they're strong enough to handle it he'll only step in if they ask him for help. If he sees something wrong, he'll say something.'

Wanganeen says the scene in *Rabbit-Proof Fence* where Gulpilil rides slowly past the girls on the porch at the Moore River Native Settlement still makes her shiver.

'That scene, every time I look at it, he knows what he's going to do, he knows. And he's ... *impressed* ... by this girl [Everlyn

Sampi's Molly], that she's doing what *we* should've done, but he can't 'cause he has ties [in the film, Moodoo's daughter is imprisoned at the Settlement]. If you look back at that scene, you can see half a smile on his face as he's looking at her. He's smiling at her! Anyone who doesn't know, he looks scary, but you can see in his eyes that he's still there. He wants to let us know. And that's our history. Most of the men in his position weren't monsters. They were kept there by people pulling on their heart strings. I'm a product of that environment and when I met Uncle David he became my teacher, and the lesson was, keep your soul calm and spirit calm and hold on to what you got.'

Years after *Rabbit-Proof Fence*, Wanganeen was in Darwin. She saw Gulpilil in a shopping mall and yelled, 'Uncle David! Hey! Hey!'

There was no response.

'He didn't recognise me. That's when he was unwell. He asked me for some money. I said, "Yeah, Uncle David. You should be right." And he wasn't, and it wasn't right. I gave him half of what I had in my pocket. He told me it was too much. I said, "You've given us enough, we have to look after you now."'

It wasn't until 2015 when Gulpilil moved to Murray Bridge, an hour-and-a-half drive on the South Eastern Freeway from Port Adelaide, and he gave up the ganja and the booze, that the friendship became something else, something deeper.

'I don't get taught the things I get taught from him,' says Wanganeen. 'He doesn't have to say anything. We just sit there and smile at each other. It's ridiculous.'

I ask Wanganeen if she speaks Yolngu Matha, Gulpilil's language.

'I speak a little bit of Yolngu. He's taught me some over the years. I pick it up. Gone an extra length to learn it so I can talk it in hospital,' she says. 'There's not many Yolngu people down here, so I find my Yolngu cousins and get them to come and talk to the Old Man. He needs to hear his language.'

Together, they talk about his movies, other movies, *their* movies, about the time he met Bruce Lee, Burt Reynolds, John Lennon, Bob Marley, Jimi Hendrix, the Queen. They're stories Gulpilil loves to tell, often with various embellishments to keep 'em fresh, and Wanganeen is a happy disciple. When it comes to Bruce Lee, Gulpilil will suddenly find a bolt of electricity and jump up and mime the little Jeet Kune Do master.

'Him being cheeky and I smile at him in awe. I didn't realise what a social butterfly Uncle David was, still is now. Mention certain things to him and his eyes light up and I can see the sixteen-year-old boy from *Walkabout*. It's so beautiful. I love watching when he comes to life. He still tries to get out and run amok. I say to him, "You need to calm down, Uncle!" You know, hearing those stories, you never thought it would be possible to do that stuff. Not just a black man, a traditional culture black man who knows his language, travelling all over the world and country *representing*.'

In 2017, Wanganeen and Gulpilil both had roles in the Netflix zombie film *Cargo*, which was filmed in South Australia's Flinders Ranges, where Gulpilil had made *The Tracker*, and starred *The Office*'s Martin Freeman.

Superficially, it's a hold-onto-your-seat story of a dystopian Australia, post-unexplained epidemic, where zombies jump out of the dark as they vigorously exercise their lust for human flesh. Cue waterfalls of pus from the undead's eyeballs and a cocktail of brown ooze from mouths.

The government has helpfully modified Fitbits the infected can wear on their wrists so they can watch the forty-eight-hour countdown from human to zombie.

The metaphor, which isn't hard to miss, is this: white man comes to Australia, destroys land, reaps what he sows. The only survivors are the Indigenous people who've gone back to their old ways in the bush.

Gulpilil plays 'The Clever Man' Daku; Wanganeen is the zombie-slayer Josie.

'They're poisoning this land, you know?' Gulpilil tells his people. 'This country, changing. It's sick. We all get sick. You get sick, too.'

White man Vic (played by archetypal Euro-Aussie, the red-head Anthony Hayes), meanwhile, represents the White Devil, the European who came and trampled Country. He is brutal, ignorant. Vic cages a little Aboriginal girl, as well as Gulpilil, to attract the flesh-eating zombies, whom he enjoys shooting.

'Fuck with me,' says Vic, pouring blood around Gulpilil's cage and tossing what is presumably meant to represent human intestines onto the cage's roof, 'and I'll fuck with you.'

Vic places a portable cassette player on the ground and cranks the music, which is I'm Talking's 1984 hit 'Trust Me', to the heavens.

'You look pretty lonely in there,' leers Vic. 'See if we can drum you up some company.'

Gulpilil, tall, upright, regal, long hair restrained by a headband, stares back at the ghastly white man.

'He was so happy on set making that film,' says Wanganeen. 'The way he is now, compared to how he was when we made *Rabbit-Proof Fence*, it didn't stop him from getting into it. Zombies, let's do it!'

Still, he needed Family. He needed Wanganeen. Just before filming began she was rushed to hospital for surgery.

'He was out on set and he called me, saying, "Where are you? You're stressing me out! I'm not going to work until you come back." When I got out of hospital he'd already left and gone back to Murray Bridge. I had to ring him up and convince him to come back. I'm his only connection down here. He was freaking. That's our bond. Our relationship is about being in each other's faces, making sure we're okay and connecting with our heart. I have a lot of uncles but, spiritually and culturally, he's my number one.'

I ask Wanganeen about the cultural baggage he's been lugging around for the past fifty years, as movie star, as traditional man.

'It's very hard for someone like him to be an icon. Everyone dresses him up to look sharp and puts him up from of stage, then they go home and nobody cares. At the screening of *Cargo*, I was on the other side of the room and when he went to get up he almost fell over. Nobody stood up to hold his hand. I put all my stuff down, ran across the room and grabbed him. He had to lean on me because he couldn't stand. They don't realise that he's not just a movie star, that he's a man as well. There are moments like that, when everyone is going, "David Gulpilil! David Gulpilil!" that I see him struggling. There's no one there for him to hold on to.'

Recently, Gulpilil and Mary visited Wanganeen in Port Adelaide for lunch, which was complemented by a homemade Pavlova dessert, Gulpilil's favourite. Wanganeen wanted to talk about her new film, *Battle of the Ancestors*, set sixty thousand years ago where various Aboriginal tribes cross each other's tribal lands and go to war.

'I asked what he wanted to put in there culturally. I needed him to tell me what he sees. He helps me work through the stories, our tongue. Our words may be different but they mean the same thing. He's helping me with my connection to my soul and my spirit. You know, we're just looking after each other.'

Wanganeen will tell Gulpilil, 'You're my shadow.'

He replies, 'You're ... *my* ... shadow.'

Did Gulpilil inspire *Battle of the Ancestors*?

'Bloody oath he did! His character, the giant crocodile, turns into a man. It's megafauna stuff. He's huge and he changes when he gets out of the water and slaps his tail.'

When Wanganeen told him about the part, he said, 'That's me! That's mine! That's my role!'

'Of course it is!' she told him. 'I wrote it for you.'

On Christmas Eve 2018, when Gulpilil was in the Royal Adelaide hospital with emphysema, Wanganeen surprised him with a teddy bear, flowers, chocolate croissants and charcoal pencils, so he could draw.

'I couldn't let you spend Christmas in hospital without a visit from me,' Wanganeen told Gulpilil.

Gulpilil peeled out his famous smile and whispered, 'My shadow, my little black shadow!'

'He's always been there for me,' says Wanganeen. 'I don't get that soul food from anywhere else. I get it from him as a man of this land, this country. We had a bonfire for his sixty-fifth birthday and I introduced him to my daughter. When she saw the photos she burst out crying. She knows she's sitting next to a teacher. What she didn't know was that Gulpilil is ... *the* ... teacher. Mummy's teacher. Just the thought of him leaving me is shattering. He tells me that I'm his apprentice and I say, "What, you're Obi Wan and I'm Luke?" He goes, "Yeah, but black one and girl."'

Wanganeen says Gulpilil has saved 'my life more than once'.

'He's dealt with being the token Aboriginal on screen. I find it very hard and the industry is more brutal these days. I get told I'm not black enough, not white enough, too short. But when it comes to culture it's different.'

Wanganeen will ring Gulpilil and say, 'Whatcha doing? Gimme some strength!'

'You got all my strength,' he'll say.

'I tell him, "Stay strong. You're a storyteller, you're a warrior for your people. Every young Aboriginal man and woman, right now, they should say thanks, Uncle." He's the reason we're looked at differently. He showed them we're smart, we're strong, we've got culture and just because you don't understand doesn't mean it's not important. He put Aboriginal fellas on the map. He let the world know we're still here and still surviving. Sometimes he just puts his hand on my shoulder and that'll solve everything. He reminds me if he can do that, we've got a lot more that we can do for him.'

CHAPTER 13

The Handler

GULPILIL DANCED INTO THE ORBIT OF martial arts expert Wayne O'Donovan at the artists' colony Montsalvat Farm, at Christmas Hills on the outskirts of Melbourne, in the early autumn of 1991.

O'Donovan, a white fella, lived near the twenty-six-hectare property where kangaroos and wallabies still roam. He taught kickboxing to the local Koori kids and acted as cultural attaché when they got into trouble with authorities.

He'd gone to see this Indigenous dance troupe from Ramingining, featuring *Storm Boy* star David Gulpilil, fascinated by what cultural jewels they might deliver.

'I wanted to see what I was missing as an Australian,' he says.

What O'Donovan found were six Yolngu men shivering in the southern cold, all wearing shorts, T-shirts and thongs. Shocked by their unpreparedness, he went home, emptied his wardrobe of its coats and long-sleeved shirts, took 'em back in plastic bags and poured the contents at the men's feet.

A connection was forged.

For six weeks, O'Donovan drove the troupe to all their Melbourne gigs.

Two days before the dancers were due to leave Melbourne, and aware they were swamp and coastal dwellers, O'Donovan's mum, Elaine, went to the Preston Markets, bought a whole flathead, filets of trevally and gummy shark, and threw a seafood barbecue.

And it was there that Gulpilil formally asked Elaine's permission to take her son, then thirty-three, to Arnhem Land, and announced to O'Donovan that he'd be joining him in Ramingining.

O'Donovan reacted as most people would, telling Gulpilil to forget his crazy notion, that he had to work, but then he realised his excuses were as paltry as his existence felt.

'It was a major turning point in my life. I had no idea traditional Australia was still alive,' says O'Donovan, still in almost daily contact with Gulpilil, who calls Elaine 'Mum' to her face and 'Kortjung', his mother's skin name, when talking to other people about her.

'There was one tap and one concrete slab where fifty people, and David, lived. In the month I was there, I'd never been treated better by a group of people. They took care of me better than my own mum. It stole my heart so I decided that the best thing that I could do was to keep this Indigenous hero in front of the screen.'

For the next dozen or so years, beginning with the television series *Man from Snowy River* (1994) through to the pre-production of *Ten Canoes* (2006), O'Donovan acted as Gulpilil's handler. The role was multi-faceted. Get him to the location. Make sure he arrives on set. Attend to any personal issues. Act as a cultural attaché between director and actor.

'I was just trying to keep him out of hospital and prison, really,' he says.

O'Donovan lived in a tent with his three kids next to Gulpilil's humpy in Ramingining, camped at Gulparil for months, stayed at Gulpilil's twin sister Mary's house ('She's astonishing, ten times deadlier than David,' he says). And at the very trough of Gulpilil's life, while he was shooting the Baz Luhrmann film

Australia and living in Darwin's Long Grass bush camps with Miriam, O'Donovan was there, too.

'Through the deadly bad, the deadly good and the desperation,' says O'Donovan. 'I'd go from chasing crocodiles in deep water with him to tuxedos and first-class restaurants to wondering what we're going to kill the next day to satisfy our hunger. The contrast was huge. From being treated like royalty to be being treated like scum.'

He says the Gulpilil he found in Ramingining was more extraordinary than any character the actor played on film.

'No movie character came close to his amazing life. Two things that are unquestionable about David,' says O'Donovan. 'One, he's a master of being in front of a camera, and two, of being behind a gun. He's an exceptional hunter. He'll go all day. We'd be walking in the heat, thirty-five or so, and he wouldn't let you drink water because he said it made you tired and weak. You had to suck a pebble and you'd walk tens of kilometres, shoot dangerous animals and then carry all the bloody stuff back. I was a martial arts instructor but I felt like a Neanderthal compared to him.'

O'Donovan tells the story of walking through the middle of a billabong with Gulpilil on that first trip, thinking he was hunting turtles, when the tell-tale bubbles from a crocodile disturbed the water near him.

'Run!' shouted Gulpilil, who shot the animal as O'Donovan scrambled up into the mangroves.

'One minute I'm in Melbourne, the next I'm getting chased by a croc then killing and eating 'im,' says O'Donovan.

Whether it was because of the unfamiliar meat or the stress of being hunted by a prehistoric animal, O'Donovan became violently ill.

In the back of an old LandCruiser, Gulpilil folded his arms around him.

'I felt like I was a little kid being cuddled by Mum,' he says. 'Their duty of care makes us look shameful, really. And prior to meeting David I was a scout leader, I was training the Koori kids in kickboxing for their self-esteem, helping kids in trouble, but when I went to Arnhem Land I realised what a selfish bastard I was.

'That's the difference between the cultures. It's astonishing. And it took me by surprise. I'd never been so loved by another bloke. So I was compelled to tolerate the worst of his behaviour. I had to.'

To get a handle on Gulpilil's view of the world, it's crucial to understand he was a First Contact Indigenous man, says O'Donovan: someone who lived the first eight years of his life without seeing a Caucasian.

Gulpilil and friend Bobby Punnunr, who would accompany Gulpilil to Buckingham Palace after the success of *Walkabout* in 1971, saw a missionary seaplane land at the mouth of the Glyde River in east Arnhem Land sometime around 1961.

The pair fled, terrified.

'Remember, they weren't successfully invaded until the nineteen-seventies, only after the [1967] referendum when the missions gave up their power and a state-run community was established. It's astonishing that one of our greatest actors is a First Contact individual.'

And, to put a teenager, who'd only seen a white man for the first time a decade earlier, into the world of film in the late sixties, early seventies – well, can you imagine?

'The whole industry was sex and grog, and David thought that that extravagance in the white culture was normal; he thought that was how white fellas lived.'

This was compounded by his first minder, the actor John Meillon, who starred alongside Gulpilil in *Walkabout* and who died aged fifty-five of cirrhosis of the liver.

'It was the film industry that turned David into a drunk,' says O'Donovan. 'John Meillon was a shocking drunk. Take a seventeen-year-old from a dry country, get him on the turps. David presumed that excessive drinking was normal behaviour culturally. Alcohol was always a big problem all the way.'

Whenever O'Donovan ran into a cultural wall with Gulpilil, he'd contact the legendary Reverend Jim Downing, a social advocate who was awarded the Member of the Order of Australia for his work with Aboriginal communities, for advice.

'I'd ring him up, tell him the situation and he'd come up with an example of something similar happening in their culture and then lay their rules on it. If you tried to lay white rules on it, David wouldn't pay any attention to it; if you used their laws, it always worked. Because their laws never change, never waver, whereas white laws are constantly changing. And so there's this attitude that white man's laws are just made up. On a film shoot it's white man rules and he never knew where the boundaries were.'

Before filming for *The Tracker* began, director Rolf de Heer contacted O'Donovan to find out how he could make Gulpilil happy and comfortable for what de Heer regarded as the 'most demanding role of his career'.

'He did everything he needed for David to be culturally accommodated,' says O'Donovan. 'For the first time, David was looked after and treated like the star he is instead of this pain in the arse person the whole production had difficulty with. On other shoots where his cultural needs weren't taken into account it was surprising that David was able to survive from day to day.'

A pivotal scene in *The Tracker*, for Gulpilil, was a dance he performs when The Fugitive is spotted. For the first time on film it was a construction of his own and not a tribal dance.

'He got in big trouble for the eagle dance he does on the beach in *Storm Boy* so he was very excited to own the dance and own the song, something he didn't need permission to do,' says O'Donovan. 'Ever since *Storm Boy* he tried to keep his cultural life separate from the film industry where he'd constantly break his laws. It set up a difficult relationship that exists even today.'

During the filming of *Australia*, a nephew of Gulpilil died and a funeral was held at Ramingining. Because of his earlier transgressions against tribal law, including marrying a woman of the wrong skin (skin names represent a person's blood line), Gulpilil was so terrified he was going to be 'speared or chopped up into little bits', says O'Donovan, that he was sent as Gulpilil's proxy to fulfil the actor's role at the ceremony.

'He was paranoid about it despite me reassuring him that no one was going to get him any more. They'd all forgiven him, and because he didn't have kids with the woman, it was all right. He doubted his position at home because of all the things that he had done wrong culturally and he still carries that cultural guilt.'

O'Donovan says Gulpilil wouldn't feel safe going home.

'A lot of famous people get sick and die because of jealousies, because that other mob were jealous, so they were sung [where a sorcerer calls on the spirits to harm someone believed to have broken tribal laws]. The belief in other-world stuff is very strong. To the point that when you've been living there for a while, even if you're from the mainstream, you start experiencing and seeing things that our logic and culture can't explain; you find yourself becoming more superstitious and more susceptible to different belief systems.'

The difficulties hit Gulpilil from both cultures.

On another film, the single women on set became very attached to the glamorous Yolngu actor.

'At one stage, a gaffer in the crew was twelve inches away from my face, spitting with anger, telling me I had to keep David on a leash,' says O'Donovan. 'When it comes to dogs flirting in front of bitches, David is going to win every time. And he didn't like it.'

When that film wrapped, Gulpilil and O'Donovan split the same day, fishtailing their four-wheel-drive through the desert tracks.

'David was upset about something, relationship dynamics with other Indigenous people there. And, as we were leaving we see this other four-wheel-drive, a huge cloud, coming the other way. We pulled up, he pulled up, and it was a guy called Noel [Wilton], who'd been an extra on the film. David was saying that he was pissed off, that he wasn't looked after, and Noel was agreeing, and then David said he was going to do a new movie called *The Tracker* and that he wanted Noel to be in the movie with him. I tried to explain to David that he couldn't guarantee Noel a job. Then, when we turn up at *The Tracker*, Noel's the blooming star! He's the one that's being tracked! Everything was predetermined. That happened so often. Drove me crazy. In the mainstream, we use our clocks, our logic, our rationale, but sometimes it didn't work and whatever David said it ended up happening anyway.'

Before he met Gulpilil, O'Donovan remembers delivering a seminar on metaphysics in New York City, and someone said, 'Tell us about the Aboriginals.'

O'Donovan, surprised, said that he'd never met any Aboriginals and that we 'killed 'em all'.

Back in Sydney, where he'd moved from Melbourne, an issue of a popular weekend magazine featured a cover picture of Gulpilil, holding gun and crocodile skull, with the words, 'If anyone tries to pinch my land I'll shoot 'em!'

Inspired by an image that 'represented something about Australia I needed to learn', O'Donovan ripped the cover off the magazine and stuck it on his office noticeboard.

When he returned to Christmas Hills two years later, he took the cover with him. One week after moving back, a wind blew through his house, picked up the cover and blew it out the door, disappearing forever.

That night, he met Gulpilil at Montsalvat.

'The cover disappeared and he manifested physically. Is it a coincidence or something going down that our culture doesn't accommodate but their culture lives with? Because of things like that, I've lost faith in mainstream thinking that we all stay safe in. Seriously, when David would say something totally outrageous to me and I'd say, nah, bullshit, half the time it would come true anyway.'

The 2002 documentary *Gulpilil: One Red Blood* best explains Gulpilil's personal philosophy, says O'Donovan.

'It's not just equality between different coloured races, he was making the point that ... everything ... has red blood. We're all family and that extends to species beyond the human realm. His philosophy includes the importance of respecting and honouring plants and animals, too.'

It ain't all ethereal, however.

Every time Gulpilil met someone from overseas he would explain to them that he was a 'thoroughbred Australian' and that most other Australians, white and black, were 'mongrels'.

'And the way he explained it,' says O'Donovan, 'always had sexual overtones. I'm a thoroughbred, like a ... stallion.'

And, today?

'I've never met someone with such a capacity to go forever without sleeping, whether filming or hunting. His endurance was astonishing. That's why he's alive now even though he was supposed to have died of cancer years ago. He's like an old croc. You can shoot and wound 'em and you think you've killed 'em but they'll bite you eight hours later.'

There's a coda to that six weeks Gulpilil spent in Melbourne in 1991, a daughter born after a brief relationship with a local white woman.

Phoebe.

Put her and Gulpilil side by side and there ain't a single question of paternity. But, and there's always a but to these sorta things.

And it made his role in the Stolen Generations film, *Rabbit-Proof Fence*, particularly poignant.

'He was totally out of the loop from the beginning with Phoebe,' says O'Donovan. 'He didn't have an opportunity to have a relationship with her. Every time he came to Melbourne I'd try to line up visits, but the differences in the culture made it too hard. My ex-wife and I developed a relationship with the grandparents who raised her to let 'em know how important it was, culturally, for her to meet her aunties, these fully traditional people, these huge-hearted people.'

O'Donovan says he tried to organise meetings for seven years, from the time she was around seven, until she became a teenager and rebelled, as teenagers do, against the idea of connecting with the father she never knew.

There were moments. Small interactions.

Phoebe's grandparents took the nine-year-old to the Adelaide premiere of *The Tracker* in 2002 and to Sydney for the one-man show two years later. Plans were made by O'Donovan's wife and Phoebe's grandmother to get her to Arnhem Land so she could meet her aunties. Phoebe didn't want to go. Said she didn't feel ready.

'I tried everything I could but there was always an excuse at the last moment. Culturally, David was behind the eight ball. How was he ever going to represent himself in the Family Law Court and show how he was going to give the kid a good, middle-class life? It wouldn't have been worth it.'

While doing press for *Rabbit-Proof Fence*, O'Donovan

would pull journalists aside and tell them... *this*... is happening... *now*, Indigenous people unable to see their kids for reasons they didn't comprehend.

Children not stolen in the sense of forced removal by the State, or even willfully withheld by well-meaning parents or guardians, but blocked by cultural hurdles impossible to get over.

'While it was being filmed David kept asking, "Where's my daughter? Where's my daughter?" This is the living reality of Indigenous people, including David. Because Indigenous people are so into family, to be separated is so much worse for them than it is for a mainstreamer.'

O'Donovan wheezes in frustration. 'I felt like a failure and infuriated. I felt guilty as a white fella that I couldn't do anything.'

Clouds do part and rainbows aren't always just a play of light and water.

Gulpilil and Phoebe eventually connected in August 2016, a few months before Gulpilil's cancer diagnosis. Each week he would call his little girl until, slowly, they became comfortable with each other.

'And because there was no baggage from the past, it turned out beautifully,' he says. 'I saw Phoebe in Murray Bridge, hugging her dad, the way a little girl hugs her dad's arm with her head against it. It brought tears to my eyes. It worked out okay in the end. As a consequence of her upbringing she's highly educated, very, very smart, she looks like her Dad, and she's a shaker and mover for Indigenous people. She's only just accepted being a Gulpilil in the last twelve months and hasn't told any of her friends or work colleagues who her old man is. She's never tried to use him for kudos or status.'

The Gulpilil DNA runs deep, however.

'She's independent and stands on her own feet, ruthlessly independent like her dad. And now she's ready to deliver their culture to the mainstream.'

CHAPTER 14

A Photo Shoot at Poverty Corner

On a Thursday afternoon of twenty-six degrees, the movie star emerges from his bedroom as if fresh from a chrysalis, heavier, the curve of his back less stooped, the blue circles of his cataracts prominent.

'Hello, brother, good to see you again,' says Gulpilil, formally.

He is five kilos heavier than a few months earlier. On a man who is now sixty-four kilograms, and who got down to thirty-nine when he was in Darwin's Berrimah prison, the added ballast shows.

For the first time in months, the bones of his ribs and sternum are hidden under a layer of flesh.

The front room's electric fireplace, which remains at full power for ten months of the year, is inactive, although Gulpilil has kept his little bedroom heater burning.

Mary walks past with an empty plastic cake container in her hand, its contents having served as an after-lunch snack for the movie star.

'He's just had the last piece,' says Mary, pre-empting my next question. 'He likes his cake from Coles, sponge and strawberry.'

Gulpilil takes in the photographer standing in front of him, who has flown from Sydney to shoot an image for the cover of this book.

He smooths his hair with his hands and stands expectantly by the door.

'So I wanna take a photograph! *All right!* Let's go!'

The photographer, Richard Freeman, has identified a location for the shoot on Google Earth called Poverty Corner, fifty clicks out of town. Head northeast on the Karoonda Highway, veer left on Burdett Road towards Younghusband and turn when you see the old homestead.

It's the closet place to Murray Bridge that hasn't been bordered in trees.

Drive a few hundred metres off Burdett Road and you'll find two abandoned early-twentieth century homesteads, one with a polished wooden door handle and its decorative architraves intact, a hundred and fifty head of sheep, and one llama. The red dirt is carpeted with little round sheep droppings and pieces of bone.

During our early morning visit before bringing out the Old Man, one sheep struggles in the sand surrounding the homestead. The photographer yanks its back leg from underneath a plastic pipe and a piece of metal framing. The sheep staggers off, collapses, drags itself up and zig-zags a little further before falling on its guts. Optimism that the leg isn't broken disappears.

We grab an abandoned fuel can that has been cut in two and fill it with water from a nearby trough. The vessel is placed under the crippled sheep's snout. It'll either die out here or be shot by whomever owns the stock. The stench of shit and ammonia mixes with the dust kicked up by sheep hooves to complete a feeling of wretchedness.

A few minutes later, in another field, a sheep is stuck in a feed lot. It got in but it can't get out. The sheep, which has been shorn, bleats and struggles hopelessly. A manipulation of its hindquarters, a kick in its arse and it bounces back to its mob.

One win, one loss.

A peregrine falcon circles.

In Murray Bridge, Gulpilil is going through his wardrobe for the cover shoot, presenting various suits with a theatrical flourish.

'He's got skinny suits and fat suits,' says Mary, ''cause when he got sick he was 42.3 kilos, so he bought suits for then, then he's put on over twenty kilos... and he had to buy new suits! If he'd stayed at forty-two his body wouldn't have anything to fight with.'

On a dresser are two bottles of men's eau de toilette, Givenchy's Gentleman, which costs a hundred dollars for fifty millilitres, and a bottle of David Beckham, twenty bucks from Chemist Warehouse.

The Givenchy was a gift from his daughter-in-law and when that ran out, Mary ordered another online. It has just arrived.

Mary's smelling good, too.

Her perfume is Estée Lauder's Youth Dew, 'one of the sexiest fragrances ever created' according to its manufacturer. Top notes of rose, jonquil and lavender, a middle of jasmine and muguet with a bass line of vetiver and patchouli.

Mary says she got turned onto it at her twenty-first birthday party 'one hundred years ago when a rich old lady gave it to me'.

Apart from two uninspiring grey suits, which Gulpilil lays on his bed for us to examine, the rest of his clothes are by R.M. Williams, which he buys at a discounted rate.

'He's got one of the last R.M. Williams shirts made in Australia,' says Mary.

I express my surprise that, one, the great Australian icon charges Gulpilil, movie star, a damn cent to wear its gear and, two, that its clothes aren't fashioned by artisans in an Australian workshop.

'China,' whispers Mary. 'The Old Man would be turning in his grave.'

We pick a beige safari button-up and tell him to wear the brown pants he's got on, cinched by an R.M. Williams belt.

The photographer suddenly emerges from the walk-in wardrobe with a flashy red suit bag.

Gulpilil takes it, places it on the bed and unzips the opening.

The reveal is manna from heaven: a slim two-button, shawl-collar black suit by Jonathan Adams, recently dry-cleaned, with a silk handkerchief flowering out of its lefthand breast pocket. Gulpilil bought it from the old Ed Harry store in town for the 2017 Adelaide Film Festival where *The Tracker* played for its fifteenth anniversary.

This suit is pure Movie Star.

I tell him I want him in the suit, no shirt, no shoes.

'No worries, brother,' he says.

The photographer leaves to create a studio of sorts out in Poverty Corner.

The door slams.

A few minutes later, Gulpilil starts to shuffle impatiently.

'We're not going just yet!' says Mary.

Gulpilil heads towards the door.

'NOT JUST YET! GOTTA SET IT UP! OTHER SIDE OF TOWN!'

'Where?' he grunts.

'Half an hour!'

Another grunt.

'Where's the other R.M. Williams shirt? The one with the writing,' says Gulpilil.

'It's in the dirty wash!'
'Well, can't you get it out?'
'It's in the *dirty* wash!'
'Oh,' he says, deflated.
'*Oh*,' mimics Mary.
Mary tells me they argue a lot.
She looks at Gulpilil, laughs, and says, 'Don't we, Old Man!"
He grins back at her and nods.
'Sometimes he likes a good argument, keeps him going,' she says.
'Hang on,' says Mary, pushing herself out of her chair for the hundredth time that day and walking out of the room.
She stomps back in with the missing and yet-to-be-cleaned shirt, R.M. Williams embroidered down one of the sleeves.
'I'll iron it,' she says. 'It's not that dirty.'
Mary explains that, shortly, she'll get a local dressmaker to 'turn the collar' or unpick it, turn it upside down and restitch it, because the shirt is starting to wear and Gulpilil will 'get a little bit more out of it'.
Gulpilil gets the message that the shoot isn't happening for forty-five. He take a seat by the door. The metal chair doesn't have the generous cushioning of the arm chairs that cost twenty dollars at a junk shop, but he can get out of it easier and faster.
We all look at each other.
I ask Mary to tell me her immediate impressions when she met Gulpilil at the Darwin premiere of *Ten Canoes*.
'Kindness,' she says.
Mary had taken a middle-aged disabled man in a wheelchair to the premiere. Louie, Louis, she can't remember the name, but he was from Ramingining and had been in a chair since birth.
'David couldn't do enough to make sure he was comfortable,' says Mary.

Mary already knew Gulpilil's wife Miriam through the family of the 'incomplete paraplegic' called Jacky she was nursing and, soon, the trio became close friends.

She recalls, rocking with laughter, the time she'd gone to stay with the couple at Mandorah in Wagait Beach, eight k's west of Darwin.

'I'd locked the beer in the car and I had the keys,' says Mary. 'And this one,' pointing at Gulpilil, 'comes running out screaming, "Mary! Mary! Give us the keys! There's wild pigs running through the camp!" Do you remember that, David? If there were wild pigs he wouldn't have been standing there.'

There's an affection and intimacy between the widowed nurse Mary Hood and the movie star David Gulpilil that I'd noted in my meetings. I'd never asked straight out if they were lovers, but I hadn't been immune to their chemistry.

When the artist George Gittoes had visited, he says Gulpilil had whispered in his ear, 'This one, she's hot-blooded.'

'Of course they're lovers!' he'd boomed when I asked his opinion, further incensed by my stupidity as well as my inability, thus far, to engineer a trip back to Ramingining for Gulpilil.

Today I ask Mary: Is this a love story?

'NO!' she hoots, floored by the suggestion.

It would make a great storyline, I tell her, the Movie Star and the Nurse.

'No, no, no,' she says.

I know you take caring for him seriously, I say.

'I do,' she says, softly. 'Yeah. Miriam always says to me when she rings up, you keep Old Man down there and look after him. Look after him properly nanna. She's not well herself. We're all getting older and sicker.'

Are Miriam and Gulpilil still married?

'In their own way, yeah.'

The playwright Reg Cribb told me that Miriam is a hell of a

performer and, one night, he saw her own a stage, overshadowing even Gulpilil.

'She's got a really sweet voice,' says Mary. 'And, she's really clever. When her people went out hunting, even if they didn't catch anything, she always got a feed.'

When you lived in Darwin and the pair were still on the booze, was it hard to see them drink?

Mary relates it to Gulpilil's relationship with piss now, sober for half-a-dozen years.

'I overreacted one night,' she says. 'One of his kids was here and we'd been out to tea and she'd had a little too much to drink and he was telling her to go away. He couldn't stand it. I absolutely cracked it. I had flashbacks.'

Gulpilil re-enters the scene, his hair pulled tight back across his head.

'Here? Like this?' he says proudly.

He does look good.

'He put the brush through it,' says Mary.

When Gulpilil copped a year in prison for the aggravated assault of his wife Miriam in 2011, Mary was one of the few people who came to visit.

'Rolf went, Miriam went a couple of times, that's about all,' says Mary.

Why?

'Darwin.'

Mary huffs, a pointer to her frustration and sadness.

'The people of Darwin were never very kind to him. *Never*. I didn't really realise it until we went down to Tennant Creek once and not one person humbugged him. They were all grateful he was there. In Darwin, it's *gimme gimme gimme*. I've had him sitting in the front of a car with a six-pack in his lap and there's all these hands coming in through the window trying to grab 'em.'

'Take this, ay?' says Gulpilil, holding a black plastic brush.

Mary fumes on the earlier theme.

'And the cigarettes! *Gimme gimme gimme!* He used to keep them in my bag and then I saw someone diving in my bag.'

We talk about Gulpilil's health.

'He hasn't had a chest infection for a while. What they think was happening – because he had some really funny bugs in his right lung – was he'd nod off with food in his mouth and it goes into his right lung. And then I realised, we'd get somewhere after he'd fallen asleep and there was chocolate from his Magnum everywhere.'

Gulpilil likes Magnums, the luxurious four-dollar ice-cream treat created by a Belgian chocolatier thirty years ago.

When he was on the steroid Prednisolone, Mary says she couldn't get enough food into him.

'It was three meals a day plus five Magnums, a couple of pies, milkshakes, wasn't it David! And Coke! There's seven in there still. He likes McDonald's, too, Filet-O-Fish, isn't it! And hotcakes! And what did you have from Hungry Jack's the other day, a Whopper or something?'

Most days, Gulpilil will sleep late, miss breakfast and then eat lunch and dinner, always mullet or butterfly fish and chips, now that barramundi has disappeared off the menu at the Swanport, where best pal Terry is back working after his brief retirement from the kitchen there.

It gets expensive for two pensioners. The mains are twenty bucks each, plus the Cokes plus the cups of tea. And the meal is repeated twice a day.

'Oh well, he can spend it on himself, can't you Ol' Man! You can spend it on yourself, ay?'

Mary told Gulpilil a thriftier way of dealing with his Magnum and Coke addiction would be to buy 'em by the carton.

'I've come to the conclusion that it's not so much the ice

cream or the Coke or the pie it's getting out of the house to get something.'

Gulpilil may have lost the animation that put cinema patrons into rapture, but he still digs meeting people, being outside, breathing clean air, seeing the sky, watching the birds circle, feeling whatever sun is there on his face, the changing seasons of the land, his land.

The following week, says Mary, documentary-maker Molly Reynolds has arranged a meeting between Gulpilil and a Maasai Warrior called Joseph.

'Down at (friends) Cheryl and Bob's,' says Mary. 'They've got this place called Elephant's Rest. They go to Africa every year and they've been adopted by the Maasai tribe. Molly wants to film David meeting Joseph.'

Joseph the Maasai Warrior, meet Gulpilil, dancer, singer, artist, movie star.

———

Mary is up. Gulpilil has his walking stick in his fist.

'We go, now we go,' he says.

Mary's car is a fifteen-year-old, two-door Hyundai Getz, in battleship silver, which she bought for four gees and with only seventy-five thousand k's on the clock.

The previous owner never took it further than Tailem Bend, explains Mary, as I climb into the back and Gulpilil into the passenger seat.

At the end of the battle-axe block, three kids wave at Gulpilil, who sits low in his seat and returns with a regal wave. Mary turns on the stereo.

Post Malone's 'Better Now' fills the car as we drive along Murray Bridge's main drag, Adelaide Drive.

A red Commodore pulls up beside the Getz at the traffic lights.

All the windows are down. Two kids in the back stare at the movie star; mum, whose arm is tattooed from elbow to hand, flashes a wide smile.

Maybe they saw Gulpilil's cameo in the new *Storm Boy*. Or as Jagamarra, the sage grandfather who teaches the cute kid Pete the old ways, in *Satellite Boy*.

There's a joyful note in their reaction. Respect. Gratitude.

Gulpilil stares ahead.

The only movement is the stub of his left index finger on the electric window button. Up.

Silence.

As we hit the Karoonda Highway, Gulpilil barks, 'How long, Mary!'

'Soon, soon,' she says.

His telephone rings. He punches the speaker button and talks loudly and expressively in Yolngu Matha.

Occasionally, he puts it down to ask, 'How long, Mary?'

In the dust bowl paddock, I help Gulpilil out of his button-up and his long-sleeved shirt; Mary swings in when it's time to swap the jeans for his suit pants.

The photographer lifts his Canon.

Step this way.

Look there.

Lift your chin.

Bring your hands to your face.

Gulpilil eats the camera alive.

He stares.

No.

Glowers.

Fierce then playful. Always strong.

A strong westerly blows his hair across his face, adding movement and drama.

Whatever the photographer needs, Gulpilil delivers.

As the sun sets, I hold his hand and walk him back to the Getz.

He refuses to leave Poverty Corner until the photographer and I have packed up all the equipment and we're safely following him and Mary to the Swanport Hotel for dinner.

The joint is thirty minutes away on Jervois Road, right there near the Murray. It's open from 8 am until 2 am daily and has forty of the latest poker machines, according to its promotional literature.

Inside, Gulpilil chooses grilled mullet with chips for eighteen dollars while Mary fixes him a small bowl of vegetables from the salad buffet. I buy him the obligatory Coke to match his cup of tea and glass of water.

Mary takes a beef schnitzel that appears to've been cut from an entire side of beef, with a side of mash instead of chips.

Small talk over dinner.

Gulpilil says he prefers acting to writing and that *Charlie's Country,* which he co-wrote with Rolf de Heer, was punched out over a couple of months.

When he gets up to leave, Terry Hocking comes out of the kitchen, playfully spins him around and makes a farting sound.

Gulpilil smiles and lifts his arm, the action revealing a silver bracelet. It was a sixty-fifth birthday gift from Terry, although Gulpilil had taken it off in hospital a few months back because the metal felt too cold next to his skin.

Earlier that morning, he had seen it in his bedside draw. Mary clipped it back onto a wrist even her little fingers can encircle.

It reads: *Friends Forever.*

The following morning, the photographer and I come back for a few shots inside the house.

I sit down with Mary.

Do you ever think about life without Gulpilil?

'At times, yeah.'

'Mary!' Gulpilil yells from the bedroom.

'As Molly [Reynolds] said, I have to find something to fill my time in.'

'My heart.'

'Slow down, slow down,' says Mary, calmly.

'Yeah, yeah,' panics Gulpilil, who has appeared in the doorway.

'He's getting all excited,' says Mary, returning to the life-after-Gulpilil theme. 'That's why I started painting and making the jam and chutneys.'

Does he often get heart flutters?

'He gets stressed and his heart races.'

Mary looks up at Gulpilil.

'Do you want to sit on the oxygen for a minute?'

'Yeah.'

'He had a good night's sleep last night. I find the night before he has to see the oncologist, he doesn't sleep. He's worried.'

What's causing the stress today?

'Just sometimes he gets excited.'

'MARY! MARY!'

'I'm here!'

'Mary, *please* . . .'

'Go sit on the oxygen for a minute.'

'Mary! Mary!'

We all move into Gulpilil's bedroom. He has the oxygen feeding into his nostrils. Mary finds his puffers, taking the booster end from one and putting it on the other.

Gulpilil hits it hard, punching the bottle down and inhaling deeply.

'Slowly! Not too many or your heart will start racing,' she warns.

'He does panic a bit,' she says. 'More to do with the emphysema. It's a horrible feeling. You just can't get your breath and the more you can't get your breath the more you panic and the worse it is.'

It's a confronting scene. Bedroom. Oxygen machine. Puffers. Dying man.

I ask Mary if it's okay if the photographer keeps shooting.

'He's used to it. He likes it.'

The panic disappears.

Gulpilil pulls out the tubes and heads through the kitchen.

'Going back out. Back out going,' he tells the photographer. 'Get your camera.'

Another telephone call. It's clear someone wants some cash, at least if the words 'account' and 'money' are to be judged.

It's Mary's job to transfer Gulpilil's money to whoever is chasing it. He comes in and demands to know if the transfer has been made.

'Mary!'

'They mightn't get it until tomorrow! I've sent it!'

Does he still get hassled for money?

'Yes and it's a bone of contention between us, our biggest argument,' she says. 'Some people only speak to him when they want money. They're really naughty. That causes him big stress.'

'If he ever went back to Ramingining,' says Mary, 'he'll come back with nothing. Even Rolf told him that and he knows it.'

Mary sighs.

'Ah well, never mind.'

―― CHAPTER 15 ――

A Film Critic Discusses Gulpilil's Movies

A PIXIE IN GREY FLANNEL, TWO-TONE LEATHER shoes and hair the colour of a Hollywood sun appears from the foyer of a high-rise apartment building in harbourside Sydney.

Enter the film critic Margaret Pomeranz, seventy-four, who was the breezy foil to the formal David Stratton over the course of a twenty-eight-year partnership, first on *The Movie Show* at SBS then *At the Movies* on the ABC.

Pomeranz was first turned onto Gulpilil in 1976 when she was studying screenwriting at the National Institute of Dramatic Art (NIDA) and subsequently joined the Australian Film Institute (AFI), which showed every Australian feature made that year, including *Storm Boy* and *Mad Dog Morgan*.

The spell was cast. And Pomeranz was hooked.

'That dance, that yearning love dance, outside the house in *Walkabout* is one of the great cinema moments. You know, he owns the frame because he doesn't know about it,' she says, melting into a nearby java house's microfibre two-seater couch, which I'm invited to share. 'Later, I'd realise that there wasn't a bad presence of him in any of his films. He genuinely loves the audience and the camera loves him too.'

At one point in the early 2000s, with Gulpilil living in a humpy and with his LandCruiser inoperable, Pomeranz tried to organise a free car from Toyota for the actor she so admired.

'He was living on the other side of the river and he didn't have a car and I went all out to try and organise Toyota to give him a LandCruiser. He was so iconic and in need of our support. You go through periods in your life when you're down and out and he felt that he was owed something by his community. And I thought he was too. I also thought that a giant corporation like Toyota could give him a car, even a secondhand one.'

How did that go?

The little pixie, whose blue eyes sparkle like the pool in an Esther Williams musical, throws her head back and crackles with laughter.

'Well, *no*. I put in applications and so on. But, *no*. I was a bit upset by that.'

The conversation shifts.

Do I remember the last scene in *The Tracker?*

FADE IN: Gulpilil's Tracker has killed Gary Sweet's Fanatic. The good cop, Damon Gameau's Follower, watches Gulpilil mount a horse.
Gameau: I wonder who did kill that white woman?
Gulpilil: Probably white fella, boss! They are murderers! Shifty! Thieving! Dishonest mob! Can't trust 'em one bit.
Fade out to Gulpilil's laughter.

'That *line* at the end,' says Pomeranz. 'It's such a sweet ending. When I watch David I feel this huge affection and gratitude. I love cinema and I think he's given something to me from his presence on screen. That means something to me. And it's not just his screen presence, it's also that mystery in him. He's charming, he's adorable. And it's not just talent. It's the man himself. There is no one like David Gulpilil in film. Anywhere in the world. He's absolutely unique. To put him into any sort of category seems absurd.'

In 2015, Pomeranz was engaged to interview Gulpilil on stage in Melbourne at the release of Molly Reynolds' harrowing documentary about Ramingining, *Another Country*, which Gulpilil narrated.

It wasn't the first time the pair had appeared on stage. In 2004, Pomeranz interviewed Gulpilil for *Message Sticks*, an annual showcase of Indigenous art and culture at the Sydney Opera House.

'I have this image of him during *Message Sticks* just *performing*. He performs when you interview him. He uses his body when he's talking and I love that image of him in that moment. And that face, that unforgettable face. It was truly magical because he was so unpredictable and funny and informative.'

The hour-long interview in Melbourne, eleven years later, veered between high comedy, train wreck and moments where it feels a knife is being driven into your heart.

At one point, Gulpilil, who was outfitted in a grey suit, cowboy tie and spectacles, stood and described meeting the Queen in 1971 at Buckingham Palace.

The mimic came out.

'A kid standing there asked the Queen [in excellent regal accent], *"Does that ... Aborigine ... have a tail?"*

'No, that's a kangaroo!' hooted Gulpilil.

The crowd laughed.

Pomeranz asked Gulpilil about director Rolf de Heer finding him in jail, emaciated and alone – the event that would later form part of *Charlie's Country*.

'He'd been living in the Long Grass in Darwin,' says Pomeranz. 'He was lost and drunk and for him to be thirty-nine kilos, well, I mean, hell. It was just horrible. And when I asked him about it he got very upset. I really blame myself for asking. But I think

Rolf making that film was lifesaving. Rolf was heroic, living down in Tasmania, getting on a plane, going all the way up there, realising that he had to do something for this man and the one thing he could do was make a film.'

Gulpilil visibly shrank at the question on stage. His arms closed protectively around his body.

'I cry. I cried in my heart,' says Gulpilil. '[Rolf] said, "Where are you going from here?" I don't know. Same place.'

Gulpilil held his microphone and began to weep.

'My heart cry, here. In front of you. When Rolf came, "Where you wanna go?" I said, "We make film." I believe I dream in my brain. I was ready to die. *Charlie's Country* saved my life. And saved my people's life.'

'I think that when the first bit of notoriety faded [after his run of films in the seventies and eighties] he was lost,' says Pomeranz. 'He got used to being feted. He likes being feted and it's so hard to be feted and then, suddenly, ignored. Certainly, in later films, that came back to him.'

Before the interview, Pomeranz says an arts editor at one of the major newspapers had told her that Gulpilil was 'really rambling' and wished her a sardonic 'good luck with it'.

'But, you gotta hand it to him, he comes to the party,' says Pomeranz. 'And it was real. I got so touched by this huge audience. The camerawoman came up afterwards and wanted to embrace him.'

Two years later, Pomeranz was at the Adelaide premiere of the post-apocalypse zombie flick, *Cargo*.

'I was sitting next to this guy who was one of the program writers and I saw David on the screen and he looked really healthy!' says Pomeranz. 'And I went, "Isn't that great!" And he said, "You know he's dying."'

Pomeranz says she was 'absolutely floored.'

Later, she went up to Gulpilil, but his cataracts got in the way.

'David's sight was so bad he didn't recognise me,' says Pomeranz. 'I had to hold on to him and say, "It's ME!"'

I ask Pomeranz to describe the moment when Gulpilil realised who the woman with the chicly coiffured beach-boy haircut was.

A girlish laugh. 'You know, the *smile*.'

As a film critic, do you believe Australian filmmakers have used Gulpilil well? Could he have been cast as something other than a tracker or a bush boy?

'Australia has changed enormously over the last twenty years so that we're embracing our multiculturalism much more than we ever did. I know that when SBS first started [in 1980], Aboriginal material was a no-go area. It didn't rate. It was felt people didn't want to watch it ... But when you think about the films, what was he going to be in a *Rabbit-Proof Fence* except a tracker? *Charlie's Country*? That's basically him.'

Pomeranz says she'll remember Gulpilil for his 'magic on screen', obviously, but also because, 'I grew up in white bread Australia and having access to Indigenous people and Indigenous culture has been a privilege. He was the beginning of Australia's reconciliation with our Indigenous people. He represented that connection with the land that white Australia hadn't really embraced except to exploit it for money.'

Speaking of money, Pomeranz asks how Gulpilil's doing.

I tell her he could always do with a little cash.

After each visit to Murray Bridge, Gulpilil would light up my phone wanting to know when I'd be back.

At first I was flattered.

Then, as the calls became more insistent, I asked, 'Brother, do you need some money?'

He'd say, 'Yeah, yeah, I'm broke,' or 'Yeah, my rego's due.'

Or some other variation.

At one point, I overheard Mary yelling, 'David, you have three twenty-nine in your account!'

I didn't know whether it was three bucks or three hundred. Either way, he wasn't living in a world of private jets and Bentleys.

'Send him some money, if you can,' I tell Pomeranz. 'Even a hundred bucks.'

Pomeranz swings the door open to her apartment building.

'Oh, it'll be a lot more than that,' she winks.

CHAPTER 16

From Dreams to Nightmares

RICHARD TRUDGEN, WHOSE SEMINAL BOOK *Why Warriors Lie Down and Die*, helped me unlock Gulpilil, movie star, doesn't butter his words.

'David was a great disappointment to his parents,' he says.

Trudgen tells the story of seeing Gulpilil in Darwin – must've been around 1978, just after Peter Weir's *The Last Wave*, maybe.

Gulpilil had a wad of cash in his fist.

He peeled off $32,000 and handed Trudgen the colourful roll.

'Give this to my mother,' he said.

Trudgen looked at the even bigger stack in Gulpilil's hand and said, 'What are you going to do with that?'

Gulpilil whooped. 'Gonna have a party!'

'I don't know who convinced him it was better to get cash. Somebody... some... *idiot*... convinced him, I'd say a producer that didn't mind taking royalties for the rest of his life, and he just swallowed it,' says Trudgen.

'I talked about it to him a number of times. I said, "Look, make me your manager and I tell you what, you'll have some money for the rest of your life." And he said, "No! No way! Better off to get the money!"

'Well!...'

The memory winds Trudgen tight. Lips purse in frustration.

He fires a machine-gun staccato, '*Ffft... ffft... ffft...*

'That's the trouble with so many agreements with Aboriginal people where they don't get the full story given to them,' he says. 'People rip them off and he was getting ripped off big time.'

Trudgen, a white fella, was a twenty-three-year-old fitter and turner in 1973 when he moved from Canowindra in central New South Wales to Galiwin'ku on Elcho Island in northeast Arnhem Land. Fascinated by the people, he switched to community work, basic grammar and pronunciation of Yolngu Matha via cassette tapes, conversational speech through his everyday interactions, and he studied Yolngu history as well as its sophisticated societal framework called the *Madayin*.

'There is no equivalent for Madayin in English as it compasses a whole system of law and living,' he'd write a quarter of a century later in *Why Warriors Lie Down and Die*.

It included:

> ... all the property resource, criminal, economic, moral and religious laws of the people ... the trading highways that criss-cross Arnhem Land ... the embassy sites on close and distant clan estates that give travellers and traders protection at law ... the protected production sites (hatcheries and nurseries) for different animals, fish and birds ... diplomatic rules and regulations throughout all the clans and nations.

It was seen 'as holy, demanding great respect ... it is this tranquil state, where every clan member can live in freedom from hostility or threat of oppression'.

A passionate and driven man who saw the ineffectiveness of government and mission programs, Trudgen pushed for an approach where Yolngu worked within their own laws and social structure.

People thought he was nuts.

'What he said seemed strange to many Balanda and even to some of us mission-educated Yolnu because we did not see our own confusion,' writes Rev. Dr Djiniyini Gondarra, OAM, in the foreword to *Why Warriors Lie Down and Die*. 'Only the old men... understood him. Many Balanda considered he was *bawa'mirr* (mad)... From all the pressure, [he] became very sick and in 1983 left Arnhem Land after eleven years.'

Trudgen was stretchered out of Arnhem Land, close to death, after contracting a golden staph infection. He went back in 1992 at the insistence of Gondarra and the chairman and director of Aboriginal Resource and Development Services (ARDS).

He says his return to work with the Yolngu 'was marked by the stark reality of what had become "normal life" in Arnhem Land'.

The people, he wrote, were dying prematurely at a 'horrific rate'. More than five times the national average. And dying of the so-called affluent diseases – heart attacks, cancer, stroke and diabetes – that had previously been the mark of Western societies who lived on sugar-soaked foods that came in boxes and tins.

Jobs, meanwhile, had become non-existent.

When Trudgen left Arnhem Land, almost all work was carried out by Yolngu. When he returned, only a few had meaningful work.

'As one male community member said to me in 1997, "Brother, I have not had a job since you left here in 1983... there is no work here for Yolngu; there is only work for outsiders."'

The central economic activity for Yolngu was getting the dole. Which led to the welfare cycle of dependency and hopelessness.

'And hopelessness in turn translates into destructive social behaviour – neglect of responsibility, drug abuse, violence, self-abuse, homicide, incest and suicide,' writes Trudgen. 'How is it that Yolngu, who once enjoyed excellent health, resilient social stability and an economic system that stimulated international trade into what today is Indonesia, now find themselves in this demoralised state?'

Why Warriors Lie Down and Die was written as a textbook to explain why the Aboriginal people of Arnhem Land 'face the greatest crisis in health and education since European contact' and how to solve it. Gondarra writes:

> Many books and papers have been written about the Yolngu of Arnhem Land. This one is very different. It is written out of the pain experienced by living with the suffering that is everyday life for Yolngu. But [Trudgen] has not stopped there. Out of this pain has grown something very valuable in the form of new understandings and a new way for Yolngu to learn about the foreign Balanda world.

On the cover of *Why Warriors Lie Down and Die*, which is onto its eleventh printing, is Witiyana Marika, the man who'll sing Gulpilil's spirit into the next world and who replaced Gulpilil on the Jack Thompson film, *High Ground*.

The great circle of life continues.

Trudgen is now sixty-nine and lives at Nhulunbuy on the Gove Peninsula. He produces videos, lessons and podcasts on his website djambatjmarram.com to help Yolngu understand everything from business invoices to how government debt works.

He is one of the few people still alive who knew Gulpilil's parents.

Gulpilil's father, he says, died some time in 1977 or 1978, lived a traditional life in the bush and was killed by gangrene due to his belief in the infallibility of Western medicine.

'Blood poisoning of the whole body,' says Trudgen. 'And it was caused by reusing Balanda bandages. Now, traditionally, people used to use the bush bandages, which is bark from the paperbark tree, which has [the natural antiseptic] tea tree oil. The problem was... *is*... the white fella medicine got seen as sophisticated medicine. And that occurred because people had the experience with Penicillin, and the same thing occurred across the world from Africa to South America, where it was seen as a magic drug that came out of a bottle white fellas had. They had no other knowledge of it. They didn't know if it came from a special spring or came from wherever, but it was extremely effective in curing some of the bacterial infections people had in their lives. And so bandages were seen in the same way – one-shot magic medicine.

'His father got a very bad infection, went gangrene, they took him to Elcho and I remember him sending messages through the radio service, to me at Ramingining. He kept asking me whether I could find David and David was up at Goulburn Island or something. I had three or four messages sent there, telling him to come back and see his father before his father passed away. I'm pretty sure he got the messages, but for some reason he didn't respond.'

How old was Gulpilil's father?

'I have no idea at all. He probably didn't know how old he was either. Could've been pushing eighty, ninety. People lived to a very old age, traditionally, not like today. It's very hard to work out their date of birth.'

The best you can do to determine someone's age, says Trudgen, is to ask 'em whether they were born before or after this person or that person. It's a ball-park figure.

As for Gulpilil's father's name, Trudgen can't remember

it. Too far back in time to snatch from the faded credits in his memory. (Gulpilil will tell me later it was Djinangdjo.)

He does remember Gulpilil's mother. Her name was Bunapiy, which is the Yolngu word for tree bend.

Bunapiy had lost a leg to leprosy and had spent time at the East Arm Leprosarium in Darwin where she was fitted with a wooden prosthetic. Despite the handicap, says Trudgen, it didn't dull her spirit.

'An incredible woman, absolutely incredible,' he says. 'Even with her wooden leg I couldn't keep up with her. She was very traditional. She was a resourceful lady and very skilled in the bush.'

Trudgen's job was 'homeland development' and after the death of Gulpilil's father, he worked with Bunapiy to have an airport built at Banabang-ngura, her paternal grandmother's country.

'Across the other side of the swamp from Ramingining. Terribly isolated. They were one of the most isolated groups of people in Australia. Once the rain came we couldn't get to them. I spent many years with her trying to get an airport over there. I walked over the country, marked out the airport, all that stuff to get the planes in there.'

I ask Trudgen what the goal of homeland development was.

A dumb question? He laughs.

'It was people wanting to be on their country,' he says. 'Because when they moved, just take Bunapiy for example, when she and her sisters moved into Ramingining they became dependent on the white fellas: their store, their money, their everything. When they were on their land there was no dependency. They just knew where to go, what to do. They had a high level of mastery of survival in the bush. And they were at home. They just loved it.'

The problem was that all the traditional trading routes had

been destroyed by European pastoralists, by their animals, their farming methods and, over the course of fifty years and four 'pastoral wars', their guns.

The Yolngu's extensive international trade with Macassar in southern Sulawesi evaporated in 1906 when the South Australian government pulled the licences for the Macassans to fish for trepang in Australian waters.

Boomerangs, for example, came from central Australia; fish hooks, fishing lines, bolts of calico, steel, came from Macassar.

Then, nothing.

'The great trading tracks in Australia collapsed as the whites' civilisation went out and destroyed traditional homelands and wiped out tribes across the country. People were dependent on trade for thousands of years,' says Trudgen.

'Things that were produced by high-skilled people in countries or estates that were hundreds of kilometres away. Those objects used to move up and down the trading tracks. So, what the old people told to me, starting in the nineteen-twenties, thirties, forties, there were no goods coming through that could be traded. And so they didn't have enough to be able to survive.

'And the homeland movement was to help people get back onto their estate where they were self-sufficient, very healthy, extremely healthy; weren't living in a dependent situation; and hopefully move them towards what was seen as the steps of development: get a school in there, some sort of good communication system, a good airstrip, good water, and a radio service so they can call for help.'

These days, Banabang-ngura is deserted.

'There's nobody there because there was no one looking after them after the death of a senior elder in the group who was the main male provider of big animals, goods and the protection of the women,' says Trudgen. 'Bunapiy struggled terribly. So they all ended up at Ramingining, living in dependency.'

Bunapiy died during Trudgen's eight years away from Arnhem Land.

'One of the sad aspects for me was the homeland movement wasn't picked up by other people when I went out on a stretcher.'

I ask Trudgen how Bunapiy died.

Trudgen whispers.

'Probably a broken heart.'

Trudgen says his relationship with David Gulpilil was never easy.

'David wouldn't listen to me,' he says. 'I worked on what we call the mission, right? And he had the world view that missionaries were all bad, they were all doing horrible things to people's culture and it was all rubbish.'

The thing was, says Trudgen, if you wanted to work on the mission, you had to learn the language, you had to study the culture.

'We brought back ceremonies and everything else but he had this picture in his head that somehow I was the enemy and he got that out of Melbourne, the latte drinking population in Melbourne, you know? So it doesn't matter how much his mother wanted me to talk to him and help him, he just would not listen. I had him in my office quite often. As I said, after the money [when he gave Trudgen $32,000 for his mother], he wanted me to write out [government] grants. Because he'd go and talk to Charlie Perkins in Canberra, and Charlie would say, "You can get the money from the Department of Aboriginal Affairs. Just go see that bloke up there, Trudgen, get him to write out an application for you."'

Charles Perkins, OAM, was the Aboriginal activist, spokesman, freedom rider and agitator who became, in 1984, the first

Aboriginal Secretary of the Department of Aboriginal Affairs.

Perkins was also the first Aboriginal to graduate from university (1966, Bachelor of Arts, University of Sydney) and, proving he had game as an athlete, was invited to train with First Division soccer clubs Liverpool and Everton.

He quit Everton when the reserve grade manager called him a 'kangaroo bastard'.

A significant man.

'Well,' says Trudgen. 'It was all nice and lovey of Charlie to tell him those sorts of things, to set him up. It set *me* up. Here he was, down in Canberra, dressed in suits and shaking hands of all the bureaucrats and then saying to me, put an application in.'

One of the requirements of the Department of Aboriginal Affairs when it came to grants, free housing and so on, was you had to show that you were committed to living on your homeland.

'And he never lived there!' says Trudgen. 'He was living in Ramingining. We couldn't even answer the first question on the paper. And he saw me as the problem. Which is sad.'

Gulpilil's childhood was marked by relative peace, as well as excellent health, as Yolngu and the missions worked to incorporate the two cultures. Trudgen writes:

> The 'mission days' from the end of World War II until the early 1970s were in general a time of stability for the Yolngu. A few clans rebuilt their numbers and tried to come to grips with living in two worlds. By the mid to late 1950s, the Methodist Overseas Missions stations boasted the highest population growth in Australia and none of the diseases that later became chronic were evident.

'David and his whole family, men and women, they were gorgeous people. They were good lookin'! Extremely good lookin'! They stood tall and strong,' says Trudgen.

A 1948 expedition studied three major communities in Arnhem Land and found, 'The general build is athletic. Shoulders, thighs, and muscles of the vertebral column are well-developed and strong. Carriage, posture and gait are excellent... In no instance was an obese adult encountered.'

The great disappointment of Gulpilil's parents, says Trudgen, was his lack of traditional knowledge. The story he heard was that Gulpilil was twelve when he went to an eisteddfod in Darwin, blew the doors open with his preternatural talent for dance and natural beauty, and never went back to his tribal life.

'There was just no way he was going to learn all the traditional knowledge and I understand he even lost things like kinships, degrees of it. Because it just wasn't part of his practice when he was out with Europeans, talking to them all the time,' says Trudgen, describing the system of inter-relationships in Yolngu culture where real names aren't used, only one of sixteen 'skin' names.

'He could tell stories about the geese flying across the billabong, all those sorts of things, it all sounded lovely, but most of it was back in that childish view and understanding of how things worked. I think he must've been circumcised, just starting on that journey of becoming a man. But no one gets to the top of their traditional learning at twelve. You're lucky if you get there by the time you're twenty-one. Some people get there at the age of eighty.'

If Trudgen sounds a little hard on the Old Man, his tone suddenly thaws.

'It wasn't his fault. It wasn't his fault that that was the way it happened. It's just the way it is. It's like today. Kids go out to college and they come back as strangers! Absolute strangers! They become almost enemies of their own people! There's still this idea that we're *saving* Aboriginal people from themselves by going in there and dragging them out of their primitive, backward culture. They dragged David out from a beautiful place and then he ended up on the streets of Darwin.'

Was Gulpilil's contact with the West all bad?

Trudgen is dismissive.

'He was in films and all that stuff. Important to white fellas, I suppose.'

Beyond the pain of walking a cultural tightrope, I ask about Gulpilil's responsibility to slice off his earnings to his extended family and how that ruined him, financially, and the stress it put on him.

'People think he's been adopted by the white fella world. They think money is given to everybody and if you're adopted into it you can just pick it off the tree,' says Trudgen. 'So he was locked into that big time. People expected it.'

The dependency that Gulpilil's mother was forced into forty years ago is unfathomably worse now, he says.

'People are *so* much more dependent. Since The Intervention the government has created massive . . . *massive* . . . dependency. John Howard reckoned he was going to deal with welfare and dependency. And he has made the problem ten times worse!'

The Intervention was the Northern Territory National Emergency Response of 2007, in which the federal government spent almost $600 million on the compulsory acquisition of townships and creating police outposts in communities, among other measures, in response to allegations of child abuse and neglect.

'The Balanda population in those communities has doubled since The Intervention! *Doubled!* You can't just pour in that amount of money and people and think you're going to solve human problems. Because you can't. And you won't. And they haven't. They've just made it worse. It's so sad. Such a waste of resources and money. We're still leaving Yolngu, you could say, in a mystified life. They're more confused about life, now, than they've ever been.'

He does remain optimistic that it doesn't have to be this way. 'Would I be here if I didn't think I was changing people? I could be like everybody else and leave. But I know that I've changed the life of hundreds and hopefully can change the life of thousands of Yolngu... as technology advances, it gives us the chance to talk to not one or two people but up to ten thousand people at a time. Create resources where the whole community is learning. Balanda think they're saving Yolngu by getting them to a Western education system, not realising there's a traditional education system there that they're taken away from. They miss out on all that because from a Western point of view, all that traditional learning is all rubbish. A waste of time. They don't realise they're setting up these people to be just like David. To be Long Grassers for the rest of their life, moving from community to community, Balanda community to Balanda community. Not their home communities.'

Why?

'Because there are no programs to teach Yolngu English properly, especially at an academic level, so they come home feeling as though they have completely failed. As one man said to me, they come home, take off their shoes and throw 'em away and revert back to what they were before, but now they're never happy because they'll always thought they failed in breaking through to the white fella magic.'

I ask Trudgen how important it is for Gulpilil to be in Arnhem Land when he dies.

'People usually say, you've gotta be back on your Country but a lot of people are not living on Country now. They're living in what I call these refugee camps, the communities. Every time somebody dies there's massive debate about whether they were on Country or off Country. Being a spiritual person, I don't think there's any limitation for the spirit to fly across the universe. It's up to David where he wants to die.'

Is Gulpilil a tragedy?

Is his experience typical of Yolngu who attempt to walk in two cultures?

'It's typical of the colonial failure, that's what it's typical of,' says Trudgen. 'Where we use and abuse things from the traditional people and traditional culture. In this case we took a young man from his family. I don't know how long he would've lived if he'd stayed there, but he could've lived long and he could've had a better life.

'But the colonial world took him from his people and made him one of theirs. That's the sad part about it.'

CHAPTER 17

Jack Says Goodbye

IN SPITE OF HIS THRICE-A-WEEK DIALYSIS, JACK Thompson and his wife Leona make a last visit to Murray Bridge to see their old friend.

Gulpilil wears a morphine patch to manage the pain from the lung cancer and keeps nodding off during the one-hour conversation in the front room, where the heater roars despite a temperature of twenty-five degrees.

Later, Thompson will tell me that Gulpilil could hear what was going on and responded when appropriate.

'He was great, mate. He was happy. We had a cup of tea, ate little iced cakes that he calls lollies. We talked about the movie I'm making, recollections of when we first met. I was shocked by the way chemo has knocked him around physically but I was delighted by the fact that when he talked there was a bright mind still there. A lot of my peers, my contemporaries, they have to decide for themselves whether they're prepared to go through the chemo thing or just accept that now is the time to go. It's certainly bought him some extra time.'

Thompson describes Mary as a 'godsend'.

'She's in constant attendance with David, she looks after him, she's a very good companion, a *very good* companion, and his daughter often comes over from Melbourne to visit.'

His tone darkens.

'He gets humbugged for money on regular occasions. There's no doubt that David is better off where he is than up in his homeland.'

Why?

Thompson is silent for so long I think he's gone to his own Valhalla. He's thinking, seriously. Deliberating on the pros and cons of Gulpilil living out his final breaths in an unremarkable town thirty-five hundred kilometres from Marwuyu Gulparil.

'Because,' says Thompson eventually, 'in his homeland there is nothing but humbug. He's constantly subjected to it. And there's not much doubt he would wind up with nothing to his name and he'd die in the Long Grass. Whereas here, he's looked after, respected, he has some mates, he goes down the pub for lunch and he and the cook are good mates.'

Thompson delivers his verdict.

'He's certainly not an unhappy man.'

— CHAPTER 18 —

The Week Before Christmas

THE PROPRIETORS OF LAURISTON PARK, MR TERRY Hocking and Mr Michael Higginbottom, whom we identified earlier as the 'Queers on the Hill' and the 'Housewives of Monteith', have assembled a pre-Christmas Christmas dinner for Gulpilil.

Gulpilil told Hocking a few months earlier that he didn't expect to make it to Christmas and, given the shape of his lungs, one more Christmas might make it a stretch.

So let's milk this one, yeah?

Box thorns have been painted white and turned into Christmas trees. A square table is covered with a red tablecloth, each of the six guests has two antique plates decorated with drawings of native birds. Napkins have been folded into bishops' hats and placed in champagne flutes.

A lamp decorated in white Christmas ribbon, paper lanterns on nearby tables and little blue LED lights strung over mirrors and door frames create a warm glow that envelopes the table but quickly drops off, creating a sea of silhouettes, faces only coming in to relief when bent over a plate.

It is a picture of abundance and beauty that has been assembled on an op-shop budget. A display cupboard bought for thirty-five dollars, stripped back to bare wood and painted. Plates, glasses, chairs, ornaments scooped up off the side of the road or bought for pennies and lovingly repurposed.

Outside, spring has turned into summer. A palette of grey and beige has morphed into blue cloudless skies and green lawns and meticulously barbered nature strips. There's a new sheen to the sprawling town, a joint the artist George Gittoes described in the gloom of winter as having 'a puritanical emptiness'.

You can mark the seasons in Murray Bridge by Mary's right arm. She drives her silver Hyundai Getz with the window down, wing resting on the window sill.

Right now, the skin coming out of the right cigarette sleeve of her black floral dress is four shades darker, a bikini-babe brown. The rest of the canvas shivers in winter white.

Before dinner, I drive out of town, along the Murray River and past the junction of Verdun Road and Grey Street to see what sorta form Gulpilil is in. I don't expect much conversation. We're past that, or at least past attempting to squeeze words from a man for whom English has never been a pleasure to converse in. Instead, it's good to see the Old Man and sit next to him in front of a fire that rages even when the temperature is thirty degrees outside.

Gulpilil wears a purple checked button-up with a black T-shirt underneath, lightly faded R.M. Williams blue jeans, boots and his long hair is held down by a headband with an Aboriginal motif in red, black and white. He bought the headband at Strandbags in Murray Bridge while on a shopping expedition to buy a new bum bag.

'Here he comes,' says Mary.

'Whoooo,' says Gulpilil, appearing from the bedroom.

'How y'doing?'

'I'm good thank you,' he says, formally. 'I was asleep.'

'The doctors have taken him off one of the painkillers 'cause of the sleepiness,' says Mary. 'His kidneys aren't working as well as they used to and he's getting a backlog of medication. They've taken him off the [opioid] MS Contin. He had one this morning. I won't give him any more.'

We talk a little about the opening scene in *Charlie's Country*, the interaction with the cop Luke. I tell Gulpilil it gets me every time. The laughs, the pathos, the summation of black-and-white relations in Australia wrapped in a minute of dialogue.

'I'll say something for the cops up north. They're very lazy,' says Mary. 'In the community, aren't they, David. They're lazy. I know more about what's going on illegally in the community than the bloody cops that live there. Yeah. They're just lazy.'

What sort of lazy, I ask.

'Going fishing, don't they, David.'

'Yeah,' he says weakly.

Mary asks Gulpilil permission to tell a story about when he first came to Murray Bridge. They arrived home one day to find a note on the door asking Gulpilil to report to the police station immediately.

Mary rang 'em and the cops told her it was "something to do with the bank".'

Three days later, when they eventually got around to interviewing their suspect, the cops explained that an 'Aborigine man' had grabbed a woman's credit card from her while she was standing in line in the bank and had fled to the nearby bottle shop where he used it to buy booze and cigarettes.

'They showed us a photo and no way was it David,' says Mary.

'No way it was me,' says Gulpilil.

'Blind Freddie could've seen it was a desert man,' says Mary, who explained to the authorities that the distance between bank and bottle shop was too far for an invalid like Gulpilil, who has to crouch over a walking stick to make it from TV room to kitchen, to cover.

'But they said, "Someone said it looks like David."' Mary fumes. *'Well, it wasn't.'*

These sorts of accusations aren't new to Gulpilil. He's felt them his entire life.

His own regent's uncle, Edward VIII, who famously abdicated the British crown to marry the divorced American Wallis Simpson, wrote in 1920: 'They showed us some of the native Aborigines at a wayside station in the great plain yesterday afternoon, though they are the most revolting form of living creatures I've ever seen' and 'the nearest thing to monkeys I've ever seen'.

Still, in the enlightened year of 2018, surely a black man can enjoy freedom of movement without molestation from authorities.

Mary looks serious.

'Want me to tell Derek about the night we got pulled over?'

'Yes, yes. Please.'

'We got pulled over one night, driving. It was about half past eleven, twelve o'clock at night, coming home, and they tried to get me to use a breathalyser and... *I can't*... I have *never* been able to do it. Most cops are really good about it and then one of 'em points at David, who's asleep, and says, "Is he alive?"'

Mary told 'em he was and shoved Gulpilil in the ribs, telling him to wake up.

'Is he drunk?' said the cop.

Mary explained that he didn't drink.

'He looks drunk to me,' said the cop.

'And then they're carrying on about this breathalyser that I should be able to do. They worked it out that I couldn't physically do it after ten minutes. I was ready to faint. Then they asked for a licence. Not mine. *David's*. They took it, went back to the car, checked it and... nothing. I was almost asleep at the steering wheel. Next minute, I heard the licence smash down on the dashboard, they told me we could go and they shot off like a bat out of hell.'

Mary darkens at the memory.

'And that same guy was telling us the week before that his friend was working up in Ramingining. "Oh, he has a wonderful time," he said. "He goes...*fishing*!"'

Mary says she didn't complain about being hassled 'cause why bother when karma is going to spin its wheel and, besides, Gulpilil didn't want any more trouble.

Gulpilil looks at me. He wants to talk.

Mary asks him if he wants to talk about his life as a boy in Arnhem Land. About the time he brought in two score of cattle and a handful of escaped horses.

'I was working on a cattle station in east Arnhem Land as a stockman and we was moving cattle to the other station, a new station, and all the buffalo get out, you know, they really got 'em out, buffalo, hey. I run, I get the bread, squish it, damper you know, when I go down there I ask the horse, "You wanna have this?" I put the saddle back on and jump on her and go...'

How many of 'em?

'Thirty, forty, fifty cattle. Work all day and night.'

How old were you?

'I was sixteen, seventeen years old there. And, way back when I was a little boy, I used to work cleaning the horses and the cattle. We used to keep 'em in the yard all the time, move 'em around from grass to grass, and, so, one day, the cattle station didn't want 'em to be there, so we went away...yeah... yeah...me and my brother went across the border to another station.'

Gulpilil raises his left hand, the one that has the mutilated index finger.

'Drum,' he says. 'Pulled it back, hit my finger. We couldn't do nothing. We had to jump in truck and drive to Darwin and fix my finger.'

About being a dancer.

'I went to Maningrida with Dad, you got any young boys wanna dance? And they hired me for dancing and had my own dance group. One day there was the film crew. Came up from London. They said, we like to make a film with Gulpilil black boy. He can dance, sing and play. And they say, all right, so I showed them. I danced the corroboree, dancing, dancing, yes. I won the Darwin eisteddfod like that. Darwin, I won. I won them, yes. That's my life story. Every year we go to eisteddfod. I used to go there dance, from the cattle station, cattle, horses, shirt and everything off and went dancing. Darwin was a small town. Small country. I dance the heron dance. That was my dance.'

Gulpilil bends over, delicately lifts his cup of tea, drinks.

'And...'

Gulpilil laughs, *hoo hoo hoo*, suddenly lost in reverie. There's a poetry when he talks, like a Dr Seuss rhyme, a sentence repeated in inverse, paused over and examined and then rolled around out loud.

'And I was dancing, I was the best dancer. Long ago, I was the best dancer and then I play the part of a bush boy. I put my lap lap on, spear animal. When I was working in the desert [*Walkabout*], man fell down and shot himself and then he said, "C'mon, we go now." But you know he was an actor, he was the actor.'

John Meillon? When he shoots himself in front of his kids in the desert?

'John Meillon. Yeah. I got the part in *Walkabout*. For *Walkabout*. *Walkabout*.'

Mary asks, 'David, what about when you were a real little boy, before *Walkabout*?'

'When I was a little boy, I born, 1970... [thinks]...'56... [it's actually 1953, though Gulpilil can't be a hundred per cent sure, there were no birth certificates being issued in Marwuyu

Gulparil in the fifties, after all] and I was born a little boy, when I was a little boy I was born. I used to go hunting, fishing, fishing, hunting, fishing, hunting, fishing, yeah. First time I had a hunting, first time hunting, yeah. First time I was hunting...'

Who taught you to hunt?

'Fishing and the hunting, my father taught me and all his mates and all our friends. Group of people staying in Arnhem Land. Nice people. Nice people who were staying. My mother used to cook everybody yams, water lily, water lily, and my father was going hunting kangaroo, hunting kangaroo he was hunting. Kangaroo and wallaby. You won't see it! Too clever my father! Go to the river, wash him, and then we'd sit down.

'And, one day, once upon a time, one day, my father told me he climb up in this tree and he stand and throw his spear into the fish there. He stand there and climb up in the tree making sure fish can't see his shadow. Finally, I got him!'

There's a flash of animation in his eyes, despite the cataracts, despite the red veinlets, despite everything.

'Arrrgh! I went down and looked over and... "*Mum... I got the fish here*!" And she told me, "*Arrrgh, he's a good fisherman ay,*" yeah.

'And I made money... money... I made money from different people and I was a dancer, yes. I was a dancer for different people. From there I done mission station settlement and they wanted me more for television, more for television than movie. But then *The Last Wave* and then *Mad Dog Morgan*, yeah, Dennis Hopper. Me and Dennis Hopper was in that movie. And who else? Anyway, and then *Australia*, the film *Australia*, the film *Australia* with Hugh Jackman, Nicole Kidman. Yeah...'

Gulpilil shakes his head and laughs.

'Funny... *hee hee hee*... now television still want me. Now they still want me. Want me still.'

How many brothers and sisters do you have?

Mary steps in here. She says, 'You've gotta get out of our family structure and think in their family structure. It's really hard. It's not hard for them, they live it. Like, and tell me if I'm wrong David, say there's brothers. And one has a son. So, they call him father and the other two brothers a father, and they call him son. And with a daughter, say there's three sisters and they have a daughter, it's the same thing. And this is where I get stuck. If it's a woman and it's a boy they're called nephew, is that right David?'

Gulpilil nods, although unconvincingly, as if he's still lost in his earlier memories. Mary continues, using her fingers as markers.

'And, every fourth generation if it's a girl she calls her grandmother daughter and if it's a man they call him son, that's every fourth generation. Then, I've lost my train of thought now, they call the niece or the nephew, tell me if I'm wrong David, Little Auntie or Little Uncle, don't they. It's really complicated. Ours is easy!'

I call Richard Trudgen for clarification. He tells me there's no simple way to explain Yolngu family structure, although he is in the process of making an educational video on the subject.

If you really want to simplify it, think of the African adage 'It takes a village to raise a child'.

'There are no widows and no orphans,' says Trudgen. 'If one father passes away there's another father there.'

A man's nieces and nephews will all call him father.

And, a younger brother of a father might become the primary carer of a child simply because he enjoys the role more.

I ask Mary to talk about her and Gulpilil's adventures. She'd already told me about the time David jumped down a goanna hole to capture, kill and deliver its owner to a couple of girls in the Northern Territory.

Do goannas bite back?

'Yeah, they bite,' says Gulpilil.

'Tastes like chicken doesn't it, David?'

'Yeah, tastes good,' he nods.

'All of them bush tuckers are healthier than our food,' says Mary.

Do you like eating goanna and snake?

Gulpilil sits up.

'Yeah! Yeah!'

'And magpie goose,' says Mary. 'It's like a bird. I don't like it but he does. And turtle, I cooked a turtle for you once, didn't I, David? This is a bit off. That turtle was put in the oven. You and Miriam, put it in the oven. Erica, I call her daughter [Mary nursed her brother Jacky], so does David, says, "That turtle doesn't look right in the oven." I pull out the tray and it was *moving*. And she said, "Ma, it needs to be turned over and . . ."'

Mary shrieks theatrically.

'"Well . . . *you* . . . turn it over! You're the black woman! I'm not touching it!" She said, "Well, I'm not touching it."'

Mary, ever practical, found some tongs, turned it over and shoved the twitching reptile back into the oven. Then she turned to Erica and said, 'Better give it another ten minutes.'

'David reckons it was the best turtle he'd ever eaten. Didn't ya, David!'

'Yep.'

'And dugong, dugong is good for you, isn't it, David?'

'Dugong? Yeah, tastes good. So does turtle,' he says.

Mary adds that stingray made into a gluey paste is a favourite, too.

Gulpilil also enjoys kangaroo, although without teeth the animal that's served at the local Chinese can be a little tough to get through.

'But then again, he can eat a hamburger without his teeth,' says Mary.

A dinner of barramundi, seasoned with lemon pepper and cooked as a foiled parcel on the barbecue for thirty minutes, is served at Lauriston Park, along with a good twenty-dollar champagne for all the guests except Gulpilil, who enjoys the duelling pleasures of a can of Coke and a milky tea.

'Look who you're stuck next to, Mary!' says Hocking of her position adjacent to Gulpilil, adding, 'He's a beautiful man, this David.'

Hocking turns to Gulpilil.

'We gotta get David talking. Gonna sing us a song tonight, David?'

Gulpilil, who now has one of his black oilskin hats on, stares at his plate waiting for the airdrop of barbecued barramundi.

'He sings his heart out,' says Hocking, who promises to send a recording of it from her telephone. 'David? Cup of tea, all right? Coke? Tea? What else would you like?'

'Water...'

'Oh, Jesus!' hoots Hocking, 'Fish piss in water, you know!'

Hocking looks at me.

'He's thinking of something to say,' says Hocking. 'What are you doing tomorrow, David? David? *David?* You want to know? We're going out to dinner!'

'Here dinner is,' says Gulpilil as the food arrives.

Mary reaches over and spreads out the wings of the foiled parcel. Steam climbs into Gulpilil's face, pooling briefly like a cloud underneath the brim of his hat.

Dinner conversation centres around the possible repair of one of Gulpilil's walking sticks that had got caught in the spokes of his wheelchair at Royal Adelaide Hospital, Michael and Terry telling a story of flouncing around in high-heels at op shops to the shock of other patrons, and more cultural differences between black and white.

'If I bring out dessert,' says Hocking, 'all of a sudden he'll say, "Fucking bastard!" I said, "What, fucking bastard?" When I first met him I thought, oh, what a rude man, but in their lingo fucking bastard means absolutely amazing, good food! When I first met him and he said it in the restaurant, I thought, fuck, what have I done wrong.'

Eventually, Gulpilil starts shuffling, moving his chair.

'Where are you going?' asks Mary, concerned.

'I'm standing up,' says Gulpilil, irritated.

'Do you want to stay a bit longer?'

'The one person is me. I own my back and bone and foot. If I want to go, if I want to stand up, if I want to go to the toilet . . .'

It's Mary's cue to take him home.

'Sorry,' Mary whispers to me.

Gulpilil has navigated the living room in a couple of seconds and is on the veranda, where he yells, 'Mary!'

'I'm coming!' says Mary, 'I'm halfway there!'

Hocking swings alongside Gulpilil as he walks to the car.

'Going out to party are ya?'

'Nah, just going. I'm tired. Thank you for tea.'

'Glad you enjoyed it.'

'Just taking each day as it comes,' says Mary.

'I'm going to catch a goanna,' says Hocking. 'What's for lunch tomorrow? Snake?'

'Snake for lunch!' says Gulpilil, happy.

'What's for dinner?'

'Barramundi!' the trio chorus.

The silver Hyundai Getz, with Mary at the wheel although she is barely visible above the dash, starts to roll back down the driveway.

'It's not an automatic,' yells Hocking.

Mary finds a gear. The car jerks. Her arm rests on the window sill.

Gulpilil waves regally.

Hocking whispers to me Mary's conversation when the pair arrived.

'He called you an "f-ing c",' Mary had told Hocking.

Hocking then turned to Gulpilil and said, in mock exasperation, 'You called me a fucking cunt?'

'Haw, haw, I think I did,' said Gulpilil. 'I didn't mean it, brother. That was for love.'

The next morning I bang on the familiar brown metal screen door. I figure Gulpilil and I will watch one of his movies together, see what memories or thoughts it kicks up.

When I arrive at nine-thirty, Mary tells me he's been laid up on the oxygen machine. The house has the welcoming aroma of a cake being baked; in this instance it's a three-ingredient fruit cake – fruit, juice, flour.

Gulpilil carries an envelope filled with photos. We shuffle, slowly, through thirty or so photographs, some old – Gulpilil with this dance troupe at the Sydney Opera House – some of his kids when they were young, friends, a billabong, a crocodile, a brother-in-law.

The sudden lucidity from yesterday has disappeared. It's a few hours earlier than my usual visit and his emphysema means he has to fight to get oxygen into his air sacs.

I ask him what movie he wants.

'It's either *Storm Boy* or *The Tracker*,' says Mary.

'*The Tracker*?' I ask.

'Yeah, *The Tracker*?' he wheezes.

Gulpilil slumps into his armchair. Gary Sweet appears on the screen.

'Gary... Gary...' he says.

Archie Roach sings, 'But they don't know the pain in me,

'cause they can't know what I can see. I'm surrounded by misery... I like to be... always free... far away in me...'

Gulpilil is startled.

'Mary! Mary!'

'I'm here!'

Gulpilil falls back asleep.

Archie Roach sings, 'Now we're no longer free. We are dispossessed. My people, my people, my people.'

Led by Gary Sweet's character The Fanatic, a tribe of unarmed Indigenous men and women are captured, chained up and shot.

On screen, Gulpilil sing-songs to Gary Sweet, 'No such thing as an innocent black. The only innocent black is a dead black! Heee heee heeeee.'

Gulpilil twists in his chair, lifts his head. It's unclear whether he's asleep, awake or somewhere in between.

'Yeah. Now I'm retired. But I'm a legend.'

Pause.

'Australia.'

Pause.

'David Gulpilil. Australia.'

Pause.

And here, Gulpilil raises the four-and-a-half fingers of his left hand.

'Five star.'

Endnotes

CHAPTER 1 Finding Home

Page 6   'Let's talk about *Walkabout* . . .': *Gulpilil: One Red Blood*, 2002, Ronin Films.

Page 6   'It's dangerous: you might not . . .': Judith M. Kass, 'Peter Weir Interviewed by Judith M. Kass', Peter Weir Cave, 8 January 1979, http://www.peterweircave.com/articles/articlei.html.

Page 7   'He has been viewed with suspicion . . .': Reg Cribb, program notes, *Gulpilil*, 2004.

Page 7   'My friend David Gulpilil is a troubled soul . . .' Rolf de Heer, press notes for *Charlie's Country*, 2013, http://vertigoproductions.com.au/downloads/charlies_country_australian_press_kit.pdf.

CHAPTER 2 The Movie Star and the Nurse

Page 13   'In 2011, Gulpilil was sentenced to twelve months jail . . .': 'Gulpilil Jailed for Breaking Wife's Arm', ABC News, 22 September 2011, https://www.abc.net.au/news/

2011-09-22/gulpilil-sentenced-to-12-months-jail/ 2911604.

Page 14　'The women, wrote Toohey, felt excluded...': Paul Toohey, 'Long-Grassers: Indigenous Women Trade Sex for Food and Cigarettes', news.com.au, 6 May 2013, https://www.news.com.au/national/paul-toohey-darwin/news-story/9d05c8824501106d8e4423128d243afd.

Page 16　'Yolngu are taught to speak indirectly...' Richard Trudgen, *Why Warriors Lie Down and Die,* Why Warriors Pty Ltd, Nhulunbuy, 2000, p. 78.

Page 18　'One of my thoughts had been...': Rolf de Heer, press notes for *Charlie's Country,* 2013, http://vertigoproductions.com.au/downloads/charlies_country_australian_press_kit.pdf.

CHAPTER 3　My Brother Jack

Page 26　'A terrible pest to the colony...': Angela Heathcote, 'On this Day: Pemulwuy Is Killed', *Australian Geographic,* 1 June 2017, https://www.australiangeographic.com.au/blogs/on-this-day/2017/06/on-this-day-pemulwuy-is-killed.

Page 26　'The expedition's guide was the writer...': Jennifer J. Kennedy, 'Harney, William Edward (Bill) (1895–1962)', *Australian Dictionary of Biography,* National Centre of Biography, ANU, http://adb.anu.edu.au/biography/harney-william-edward-bill-10428/text18485, published first in hardcopy 1996.

Page 27   'From the moment he realized that the natives...': A.P. Elkin, introduction to *Taboo*, reproduced in 'Taboo, W.E. Harney', *The Australian Legend*, 8 December 2017, https://theaustralianlegend.wordpress.com/2017/12/08/taboo-harney.

Page 30   'Early colonists – both military and civilian...': Stephen Gapps, *The Sydney Wars, Conflict in the Early Colony 1788–1817*, NewSouth Publishing, Sydney, 2018, pp. 7–8.

CHAPTER 4 Gulpilil vs Dennis Hopper

Page 41   'setting grotesque 19th-century human behaviour...': Philippe Mora, 'The Shooting of Mad Dog Morgan', *Sydney Morning Herald*, 31 January 2010, https://www.smh.com.au/politics/federal/the-shooting-of-mad-dog-morgan-20100312-q39w.html.

Page 41   'A story in the Victorian newspaper...': Sir Solomon, 'Bloodthirsty Morgan', *The Singleton Argus*, 14 June 1924, https://trove.nla.gov.au/newspaper/article/80953125.

Page 42   'The cocaine problem in the United States...': Jahsonic, 'New Hollywood (1967–1977)', https://www.jahsonic.com/NewHollywood.html.

Page 42   'one of Hollywood's most notorious drug addicts...': Michaelangelo Matos, 'Hollywood Hellraiser Dennis Hopper Dies at 74', *Rolling Stone*, 29 May 2010, https://www.rollingstone.com/movies/movie-news/hollywood-hellraiser-dennis-hopper-dies-at-74-191659.

Page 46   'Margaret Carnegie, writer-historian...': 'Great Collector of Art and Teller of Our Tales' (obituary), *Sydney Morning Herald*, 9 August 2002, https://www.smh.com.au/national/great-collector-of-art-and-teller-of-our-tales-20020809-gdfixe.html.

Page 47   'When we finished shooting *Mad Dog Morgan*...': Philippe Mora, 'The Shooting of Mad Dog Morgan', *Sydney Morning Herald*, 31 January 2010, https://www.smh.com.au/politics/federal/the-shooting-of-mad-dog-morgan-20100312-q39w.html.

CHAPTER 6   Gulpilil Wins the Archibald

Page 66   'David is a man who crosses the lines...': Craig Ruddy, 'Archibald Prize 2004', Art Gallery of New South Wales, https://www.artgallery.nsw.gov.au/prizes/archibald/2004/27945.

Page 67   'The painter Margaret Olley supported the case...': Tracy Ong and Matthew Westwood, 'Archibald Winner Takes Prize in Court', *The Australian*, 15 June 2006, https://www.theaustralian.com.au/arts/archibald-winner-takes-prize-in-court/news-story/90e0766ed37f117879a08fdb8e3a333d.

Page 69   'Because of my conclusion that the portrait...': Natasha Wallace, 'Sketch or Painting? Judge Gives it the Brush-off', *The Age*, 15 June 2006, https://www.theage.com.au/entertainment/art-and-design/sketch-or-painting-judge-gives-it-the-brush-off-20060615-ge2irw.html.

Page 69   'It's a victory for art in general...': Natasha Wallace, 'Sketch or Painting? Judge Gives it the Brush-off', *The Age*, 15 June 2006, https://www.theage.com.au/entertainment/art-and-design/sketch-or-painting-judge-gives-it-the-brush-off-20060615-ge2irw.html.

Page 70   'I created it to make a statement...': Emily Dunn, 'Controversial and Classic up for Auction', *Sydney Morning Herald*, 25 August 2006, https://www.smh.com.au/entertainment/art-and-design/controversial-and-classic-up-for-auction-20060825-gdo92z.html.

CHAPTER 7 A Famous Artist Paints a Portrait of the Old Man

Page 79   'He requested that the portrait be my design...': 'Archibald Prize 2012', 2012, Art Gallery of New South Wales, https://www.artgallery.nsw.gov.au/prizes/archibald/2012/29244/.

Page 84   'Three years earlier, ABC Darwin had found...': Emma Masters, 'Internationally-acclaimed Actor David Gulpilil Masters Another Art Form to Share Stories', ABC News, 24 July 2015, https://www.abc.net.au/news/2015-07-07/david-gulpilil-creates-new-art/6598966.

Page 86   'I love Australia...': 'Drinkin' with Movie Stars', 26 November 2016, On the Wallaby, http://www.onthewallaby.net/?p=32.

CHAPTER 8 Paul Hogan Goes to an Alice Springs Casino, Meets Gulpilil

Page 99   'SCENE: Mick Dundee and New York reporter Sue Charlton...': Ken Shadie, John Cornell, Paul Hogan, *Crocodile Dundee* (1986).

Page 100   'This is a fascinating scene for its cultural complexities...': Paul Byrnes, 'Crocodile Dundee: Curator's notes', Australian Screen, https://aso.gov.au/titles/features/crocodile-dundee/clip2/.

CHAPTER 9 The Fanatic, The Follower and The Tracker

Page 107   'In his most substantial role since *Walkabout*...': David Stratton, 'The Tracker' (review), *Variety*, 4 March 2002, https://variety.com/2002/film/reviews/the-tracker-1200551034/.

Page 108   'Mr. Gulpilil has the mystical aura...': Stephen Holden, 'A Ballad about Hunting a Fugitive and Finding Evil', *New York Times*, 16 January 2004, http://movies2.nytimes.com/2004/01/16/movies/16TRAC.html.

Page 111   'Gary's first shot was awesome...': Rolf de Heer, production notes, *The Tracker*, 2004, https://www.vertigoproductions.com.au/downloads/Production_%20Notes_The_Tracker.pdf.

Page 113   'From the moment the British invaded Australia...': University of Newcastle, 'Colonial Frontier Massacres in Central and Eastern Australia, 1788–1930' Australian Research Council, https://c21ch.newcastle.edu.au/colonialmassacres.

CHAPTER 10 Gulpilil: The One-Man Show

Page 122   'I thought about this strange...': Angela Bennie, 'Tracking an Untamed Man of Mystery', *Sydney Morning Herald*, 8 March 2004, https://www.smh.com.au/entertainment/art-and-design/tracking-an-untamed-man-of-mystery-20040308-gdihyy.html.

Page 122   'It's been a battle...': Claire Scobie, 'King David', *Sunday Life*, 25 April 2004, https://clairescobie.com/wp-content/uploads/2014/12/250404_Gulpilils-Travels_Sunday-Life.pdf.

Page 123   'My mate Don Dunstan...': Reg Cribb, *Gulpilil*, 2004.

Page 124   'We Australians underestimate...': Tony Abbott, *Abbott As Delivered: The Defining Speeches*, edited by David Furse-Roberts and Paul Ritchie (2019).

Page 128   'When he is away from his country...': Angela Bennie, 'Tracking an Untamed Man of Mystery', *Sydney Morning Herald*, 8 March 2004, https://www.smh.com.au/entertainment/art-and-design/tracking-an-untamed-man-of-mystery-20040308-gdihyy.html.

Page 129   'One day, about eleven years ago...': Reg Cribb, *Gulpilil*, 2004.

CHAPTER 11 As Moodoo in Rabbit-Proof Fence

Page 136   'Mum would probably never have told me the story...': Doris Pilkington cited in Karl Quinn, 'Molly's Story', *Sunday Age*, 17 February 2002, quoted in Koori Web, http://www.kooriweb.org/foley/resources/film/sunage17feb02.html.

Page 136   'Gary said he didn't want any part...': Ingo Petzke, *Phillip Noyce*, Pan Macmillan, Sydney, 2004, quoted in Koori Web, http://www.kooriweb.org/foley/resources/pdfs/28.pdf.

Page 137   '[Noyce] treated the Aboriginal people as people...': Christine Olsen cited in Karl Quinn, 'Molly's Story', *Sunday Age*, 17 February 2002, quoted in Koori Web, http://www.kooriweb.org/foley/resources/film/sunage17feb02.html.

Page 137   'an extraordinary piece of storytelling by Phillip Noyce...': Paul Byrnes, 'Rabbit-Proof Fence Curator's notes', Australian Screen, https://aso.gov.au/titles/features/rabbit-proof-fence/notes.

Page 137   'The final scene of the film...': Roger Ebert, 'Rabbit-Proof Fence' (review), RogerEbert.com, 25 December 2002, https://www.rogerebert.com/reviews/rabbit-proof-fence-2002.

Page 138   'Many school teachers think...': Keith Windschuttle, 'Holes in the Rabbit-Proof Fence', *Quadrant*, 21 May 2010, https://quadrant.org.au/opinion/history-wars/2010/05/holes-in-the-rabbit-proof-fence/.

Page 138   'Noyce's sensitive dramatization...': Jamie Russell, 'Rabbit-Proof Fence' (review), BBC online, 16 October 2002, http://www.bbc.co.uk/films/2002/10/16/rabbit_proof_fence_2002_review.shtml.

Page 143   'I could see that he was frustrated...': Artfilms, *Gulpilil: One Red Blood*, DVD, 2002, https://www.artfilms.com.au/item/gulpilil-one-red-blood.

CHAPTER 12 Battle of the Ancestors

Page 150   'This practice continued until 1963...': Find & Connnect, 'South Australian Legislation, *Aborigines (Training of Children) Act 1923 (1923–37)*, 1 June 2015, https://www.findandconnect.gov.au/ref/sa/biogs/SE00265b.htm.

Page 151   'When it came to the audition for the film...': *The Age*, 29 October 2004, https://www.theage.com.au/entertainment/movies/natasha-top-of-acting-heap-20041029-gdyvzn.html.

CHAPTER 16 From Dreams to Nightmares

Page 198   'all the property resource, criminal, economic, moral and religious laws of the people...': Richard Trudgen, *Why Warriors Lie Down and Die*, Why Warriors Pty Ltd, Nhulunbuy, 2000, p. 13.

Page 199   'Only the old men...': Richard Trudgen, *Why Warriors Lie Down and Die*, Why Warriors Pty Ltd, Nhulunbuy, 2000, p. 2.

Page 199 'And hopelessness in turn translates...': Richard Trudgen, *Why Warriors Lie Down and Die*, Why Warriors Pty Ltd, Nhulunbuy, 2000, p. 7.

Page 205 'The "mission days" from the end of World War II...': Richard Trudgen, *Why Warriors Lie Down and Die*, Why Warriors Pty Ltd, Nhulunbuy, 2000, p. 43.

Page 206 'A 1948 expedition studied...': Richard Trudgen, *Why Warriors Lie Down and Die*, Why Warriors Pty Ltd, Nhulunbuy, 2000, p. 7.

CHAPTER 18 The Week Before Christmas

Page 220 'They showed us some of the native Aborigines...': https://en.wikiquote.org/wiki/Edward_VIII_of_the_United_Kingdom.

Acknowledgements

It will come as no surprise to anyone who has spun, even briefly, in David Gulpilil's orbit that this book only happened via the magic of cosmic coincidence.

To write about the mysterious actor, first, I had to find him.

My agent Jeanne Ryckmans organised a meeting with the artist, curator, activist and writer Djon Mundine OAM, a Bandjalung man now living in Sydney, with whom Gulpilil had stayed with at various points in his life.

In 1987 and through 1988, Mundine had conceived what was called the 'Aboriginal Memorial'. Two hundred hollow log coffins from Arnhem Land serpentining along a facsimile of the Glyde River commemorated Indigenous Australians who'd died because of European settlement. It was unveiled to coincide with the Australian bicentenary, one coffin for each year since 1788.

An entertaining lunch at an inner-city Sydney pub followed, although it ended with no lead to Gulpilil's whereabouts.

Shortly after, while walking down to Bondi Beach for a swim, I bumped into an actor friend, Dan Wyllie. He asked who the subject of my next book would be. I said I was chasing David Gulpilil, and that I'd just met with Djon Mundine, but the rendezvous had yielded no results.

'You better hurry,' he told me. 'Gulpy's got lung cancer.'

Wyllie explained that he'd had a small role in *Charlie's Country* and said he'd talk to its director Rolf de Heer, one of Gulpilil's closest friends.

Wyllie then told me an excellent story about Gulpilil turning up to the set of *Charlie's Country* at midday, in his Simpsons pyjamas, and barking, 'Where the fuck is Rolf?'

A day or two later, de Heer called, listened to my request and said he'd talk to Gulpilil and his carer, Mary Hood. Good to his word, something I'd soon discover defined the great Australian director, it all happened at breakneck speed.

A call, a visit and the matter was decided.

I had Gulpilil's imprimatur, now all I had to do was write it.

And, so, thank you to Jack Thompson whose theatrical flourishes were a thrill for a kid who grew up wanting to be the shearer Foley in *A Sunday Too Far Away*.

Thank you to Philippe Mora, who interrupted his sublime existence in Los Angeles and still-busy directing schedule to talk *Mad Dog Morgan*.

Thank you to Craig Ruddy, and to his partner Roberto Meza, for meeting me in a barroom and telling the story of how his iconic Archibald Prize–winning portrait *Two Worlds* came to life. And, later, agreeing to leave in the colourful parts of the interview despite some misgivings.

Thank you to the artist and documentary filmmaker George Gittoes, who flew to South Australia to paint Gulpilil's portrait and whose connection with Gulpilil was so immediate it was hard to condense his story into six thousand words.

Watching Paul Hogan smoke Winnie Blues and reminisce as he sat on a bench in his daughter's suburban frontyard was a reminder of an Australia now long gone. Thank you.

Thank you to Gary Sweet and Damon Gameau, who both starred alongside Gulpilil in *The Tracker* and whose lives were irrevocably changed by the experience.

To Reg Cribb, the writer who created the one-man show *Gulpilil*, thank you for your knowledge, your candour and for permission to run long excerpts from the remarkable show.

Thank you Terry Serio, for welcoming me into your house and recounting, with emotion and honesty, your experience as Gulpilil's handler during rehearsals for his one-man show.

Thank you to Phillip Noyce, another great Australian director, for not only agreeing to a long transcontinental telephone call, but to replying to what must have seemed like a never-ending stream of fact-checking emails.

Natasha Wanganeen, it was a pleasure to interview you and I thank you for the love you demonstrably give to Gulpilil.

Thank you to Terry O'Donovan, a crucial element of the Gulpilil story, whose own metaphysical adventures mirrored my own.

Thank you to Gulpilil's daughter Phoebe, for climbing under the deadline wire with important fact and spelling corrections.

Richard Freeman, I always love travelling with you on assignment. This book, like *Wednesdays with Bob*, wouldn't be what it is without your arresting photographs.

Margaret Pomeranz, you were as delightful and as knowledgeable about film as I'd expected. Thank you.

To Richard Trudgen, your consciousness-raising tome about Yolngu culture was an essential reference for this book. I imagine an Australia, a better Australia, where one day every school kid studies *Why Warriors Lie Down and Die*.

To Angus Fontaine, who has since moved on from his role as publisher at Pan Macmillan, thank you for suggesting Gulpilil, thank you for believing I could do the story some kind of justice and for selling the idea to your masters within the company. Thank you to John Mapps for the smooth-as-butter copy edit. To the book's proofreader, Bec Hamilton, thank you for driving a knife through the remaining mistakes and pushing me to clarify parts of the manuscript that may have left the reader in confusion. Thank you to Danielle Walker and Ingrid Ohlsson for taking the book from manuscript to printed copy, and always with humour and understanding despite so many last-minute changes. Thank you to Clare Keighery for making sure as many people as possible know this book exists. To Daniel New, thank you for the cover design.

Thank you to Lee-Ann Tjunypa Buckskin, a Narungga, Wirangu, Wotjobaluk woman, for reading the book through Indigenous Australian eyes.

Thank you Jeanne Ryckmans, my agent, who got me into the book writing and whose company, whether lunch or cocktails, never fails to dazzle.

Thank you to my parents, Cam and Kay Rielly, for the untroubled childhood, free of any sort of fear of lack of money, security and so on, which gave me the self-belief to do and be whatever I wanted. Thank you to my big brother, Grant, who was always the better writer. Thank you to my children, Shawnee, Jones and Gard. You give my life meaning and your presence creates a home. To Charlie Smith, my best friend and for the belly laughs all round, thank you.

Thank you to the fabulous, and fabulous in every sense of the word, Terry Hocking and Michael Higginbottom for your hospitality, outrageous humour and bottomless glasses of champagne.

Thank you to Rolf de Heer for giving me a window into the actor you've devoted so much of your life to, for the advice and for the wisdom. You're a precious jewel.

To Mary Hood, whose patience, stoic humour and love for Gulpilil would warm even the coldest heart, and who did everything she could to grease the wheels of this book, I can't thank you enough.

And, to Gulpilil, to whom not just me but Australia owes so much, I thank you to the stars and moon and back, brother.